A Daily Passage Through Mark

I0134540

A Daily Passage
Through Mark

John R. Wayland

A Daily Passage Through Mark
Copyright © 2004 by John R. Wayland

Whitecaps Media
P. O. Box 60385
Houston, TX 77205-0385
E-mail: whitecapsmedia@earthlink.net

Scripture taken from the NEW AMERICAN STANDARD BIBLE®,
© Copyright 1960, 1962, 1963, 1968, 1971, 1972, 1973, 1975, 1977, 1995
by The Lockman Foundation
Used by permission.
In keeping with the practice of the NASB, *small caps are used to
indicate Old Testament quotations or obvious allusions to Old
Testament texts. Furthermore, bracketed words indicate words which
are not found in the original Hebrew or Greek but [are] implied by it.*

Scripture taken from THE MESSAGE,
Copyright © by Eugene H. Peterson, 1993, 1994, 1995.
Used by permission of NavPress Publishing Group.

Cover photo © creatas.com

ISBN: 0-9750577-1-1

For information on bulk sales, contact Whitecaps Media at the
above address.

Printed in the United States of America

This devotional is dedicated to my wife, Debbie, who has pointed me to the love and grace of God for over twenty-two years.

It is also dedicated to my children, Kelly, Tyler, and Mason.

My prayer is that we would all know and love Jesus in a deeper way each day. Thanks for sticking with me in this journey of faith and service.

Contents

Preface

I LOVE THE GOSPELS. I spent sixteen years on Young Life staff explaining the life, death, and resurrection of Jesus Christ to teenagers. I did that because I wanted them to know what I knew—that Jesus Christ was worth more than their passing consideration. Jesus Christ was worth their full and undivided devotion. His love, demonstrated by His willingness to become human and die a most horrendous death for rebellious and hateful people, needs a response. His sacrificial love calls for a response of simple faith that results in steadfast following.

Now that I lead a congregation as a pastor, I find that my motivation and message is still the same. No matter how old we are or how long we have journeyed in faith with Jesus, the passages (paths made for somebody through an obstruction) we encounter *with* Him are provided *by* Him to build our faith *in* Him and strengthen our love *for* Him.

My prayer for you, as you spend time in the *written* Word of God, is that you will encounter the *living* Word of God, Jesus. The insights, lessons, and applications that make up this simple devotional developed from my own personal time with the Lord. I began to share them with my friends at Northwest Bible Church in Spring, Texas, through daily e-mails. I humbly offer them to you with the hope and prayer that God will impress upon you the insights, lessons, and applications that are needed to draw you closer to Him as well as empower you to serve Him in this dark and broken world.

I would like to acknowledge that I stand on the shoulders of some very wise and educated believers who passionately love God and His Word. John D. Grassmick's commentary on Mark's Gospel account gave me important clarity when it came to the interpretation of numerous passages. I also found great help from Charles Ryrie's notes contained in his *Study Bible*. Good and accurate *application* comes from good and accurate *interpretation*. These brothers aided me in the quest for both.

I would like to thank Sharon Trayan, Betty Hatley, and Sandy Barclay for proofreading these devotionals. Their "eye for detail" and knowledge of grammar is much appreciated by this inexperienced author who knows what he wants to say but desperately needs help in saying it properly. Any errors that remain are mine and mine alone.

I am also deeply appreciative to my friends who have been used by God to sharpen me spiritually and who have continued to encourage me as a new pastor. They include Alan Barclay, John Dingman, Mike Hotchkiss, Brent Johnson, Gabe Merrill, Lamar Schrader, and Peter Yee. Thanks, also, to the elders at Northwest Bible Church for giving me a chance to use my gifts to lead people closer to Jesus.

I owe a debt of gratitude to Marianne Spruill and Kit Sublett for making this book possible. Marianne believed in me and encouraged me that there was a broader audience for these devotionals than simply my personal e-mail list; and Kit took my words and made them into the book you now have in your hands. I am grateful to both of them.

A Daily Passage Through Mark was written in desperate dependence on the Holy Spirit of God and needs to be read the same way. I pray you are drawn closer to Jesus and that your service to Him will bring glory to Him along all of life's passages.

John Wayland
Spring, Texas

A Daily Passage Through Mark

A Voice in the Wilderness

The beginning of the gospel of Jesus Christ, the Son of God.

As it is written in Isaiah the prophet: "BEHOLD, I SEND MY MESSENGER AHEAD OF YOU, WHO WILL PREPARE YOUR WAY; THE VOICE OF ONE CRYING IN THE WILDERNESS, 'MAKE READY THE WAY OF THE LORD, MAKE HIS PATHS STRAIGHT.'" John the Baptist appeared in the wilderness preaching a baptism of repentance for the forgiveness of sins. And all the country of Judea was going out to him, and all the people of Jerusalem; and they were being baptized by him in the Jordan River, confessing their sins. John was clothed with camel's hair and [wore] a leather belt around his waist, and his diet was locusts and wild honey. And he was preaching, and saying, "After me One is coming who is mightier than I, and I am not fit to stoop down and untie the thong of His sandals. I baptized you with water; but He will baptize you with the Holy Spirit."

MARK 1:1–8

THE WILDERNESS IS a tough place to be. The wilderness in Israel, I would imagine, was an especially tough place to be. A wilderness experience is harsh in both a physical, as well as, a spiritual sense. To find oneself lost in the wilderness with an excruciating thirst and no real hope of rescue is bound to be the toughest of all places. I hope you will agree with me that it is a testimony to the love of God that He did not leave us to fend for ourselves in the spiritual wasteland many of us know as "the wilderness."

At the beginning of Mark's "good news" account of Jesus' life, we find a voice, provided by God, crying out in the midst of the spiritual wasteland with a message that *help is on the way*. But you will find in those first eight verses that people have to first admit they need and want the help. Wilderness people must come to grips with the fact that they are dying of spiritual "thirst" in the blazing heat of their desert of sin. People have to first know the diagnosis in order to make a good decision about the cure. We are shown in this passage that the disease is sin and the cure is forgiveness. John's words and work brought the people of the wilderness to the point of recognizing their disease. Jesus' words and work brought them the cure.

John was quick to point away from himself when it came to the ultimate solution to the problem of sin. We can learn a lot in these first eight verses. One of the main lessons is that Jesus Christ needs to be the focus of our *attention* and *discussion* when it comes to "the cure." The cure is not in us. The spiritual thirst we see around us can only be quenched by Jesus. Let's follow John's example and point our friends to the One "who is mightier than" . . . us!

The wilderness is a tough place to be. We all have friends who are dying in that wilderness. Let's give them the same chance we had to face the tough diagnosis, knowing that the cure is at hand. There is a great need today for a "voice of one crying in the wilderness." Don't let yours be silent.

To Feel His Pleasure

In those days Jesus came from Nazareth in Galilee and was baptized by John in the Jordan. Immediately coming up out of the water, He saw the heavens opening, and the Spirit like a dove descending upon Him; and a voice came out of the heavens: "You are My beloved Son, in You I am well-pleased."

MARK 1:9–11

CAN YOU HONESTLY say that you feel the pleasure of God on your life? If not, what do you think it would take to feel His pleasure? Jesus felt the pleasure of His Father as He went from the obedience of baptism to the obedience of a wilderness experience.

Jesus' baptism was an act of obedience as He followed His Father's desire for Him to connect to the human race. It just so happens Jesus' favorite title for Himself was "Son of Man." In other words, I believe He loved, to the extreme, His assignment to connect even though it meant His dying to self and taking on the will of His Father. His obedience took Him all the way from baptism (where He felt the pleasure of God) to the cross, where He was forced to feel the wrath of God.

Jesus definitely heard His Father's voice when He came out of the water. I wish I had been there to hear that booming voice from heaven. Apparently some folks mistook it for thunder. Though the people around Jesus were confused, I am convinced Jesus was not. I am convinced He heard His Father say loud and clear, "You are My beloved Son, in You I am well-pleased."

Wow! To hear that God is pleased with you and me and that we are His beloved! What does it take to hear that? What must you and I do to hear that wonderful message? What does it take to *feel* the pleasure of God? It takes obedience!

Simply stated, receiving our marching orders and following

them leads to knowing the pleasure of God. Doing as we are told, no questions asked. The Scriptures tell us that God is pleased by faith in action. Faith in action is another way of saying obedience. It is this obedience that leads to knowing, first hand, God's pleasure.

What have you been asked to do today by your Heavenly Father? What is being left undone on your part? I assure you, the voice you and I hear giving our marching orders will be the same voice we hear saying, ". . . in you I am well pleased." Obey the thundering voice and you will hear the thundering voice . . . expressing His pleasure!

As the Battle Rages

Immediately the Spirit impelled Him [to] [go] out into
the wilderness. And He was in the wilderness forty days
being tempted by Satan; and He was with the wild beasts,
and the angels were ministering to Him.

MARK 1:12–13

WHAT'S YOUR POISON? What tempts you more than anything else?
You'd better be able to answer that question for yourself because
I assure you Satan knows. The enemy's goal is to tempt you and
me into failure. His goal is to knock you and me out of the race
by tempting us to quit running. So I ask you again, what's your
poison?

Some of us are weak in the area of pride. We are tempted to
take the credit when we know it belongs to someone else. Pride is a
huge stumbling block for many of us who follow Jesus because we
stop thanking the Lord and start thanking ourselves. Some of us
are tempted to drink too much alcohol. If the enemy can get us to
be controlled by a chemical rather than the Spirit, he wins. The list
is almost endless . . .

Sex, quarrelling, rage, fear, control, busyness, enmity, strife, fac-
tions—all are on the table when it comes to options for the enemy.

Believe it or not, Jesus' trek to the wilderness was God's will. It
was the staging ground for a tremendous battle. Jesus was tempted
for forty days and I assure you the battle was fierce. I can also assure you that He did not fight the battle in His flesh. The details
of His temptation are given in the other Gospels. Read them and
you will find that Jesus was tempted to not trust God's *provision*
(by turning stones to bread), God's *providence* (by bowing the knee
to Satan), and to test God's *protection* (by jumping and watching
God send in the angels). Jesus would have won so many people to
Himself—they would have been impressed—if He had taken the

5

"poison" offered ... but it would have been apart from the cross. He was tempted to have it all by avoiding the pain of execution by crucifixion. As the battle raged, He depended on His Father and He used the truth of God's Word to fight back.

"Lead us not into temptation" is how Jesus asks us to pray. Because God cannot tempt us with evil (James 1:13), I have begun to ask God not to allow an *opportunity to sin* to happen at the same time I have an *urge to sin*. As a result, I often find that I have an opportunity to sin and yet I do not have the urge. At other times, I find that I have an urge to sin but do not have the opportunity. When the two happen at the same time, I am reminded to take God *at* His word as revealed *in* His Word. Like Jesus did.

Even though there will be many opportunities for the enemy to tempt us with our "poison" throughout the day, there is no reason we have to give in. You and I have the very God of the universe inside of us, fighting for us. We have the Word of God as our sword in this fight. Since we know Who wins in the very end, let's let Him have His way now ... even as the battle rages.

The Message Must Get Through

Now after John had been taken into custody, Jesus came into Galilee, preaching the gospel of God, and saying, "The time is fulfilled, and the kingdom of God is at hand; repent and believe in the gospel."

MARK 1:14–15

TAKE A CAREFUL look at the facts in these two verses. We see the *arrest* of the "voice of one crying in the wilderness," the *arrival* of the Son of God, the *announcement* of the gospel of God, the *approach* of the kingdom of God, and a call to *accept* the "Good News" by faith.

No matter how hard the opposition tried to silence the message of God's passionate pursuit of His creation, the message got through. They arrested John with the hope that "the voice" would be silenced, but then Jesus Himself came into the spiritual wasteland telling the truth about God's love and grace. Jesus shared that good news by both His words and works because that message needed to get through to people who were then (and are today) in deep spiritual need. It was (and is) the news that a wayward creation was being pursued by its loving and powerful Creator.

The news that needed to get through was that citizens of a fallen kingdom run by fallen men in a fallen world could be translated into a new and perfect kingdom run by the perfect King of kings. That kingdom was approaching and those who desired to "immigrate" needed only accept the offer by faith.

They were used to the notion that it was something they would have to earn. They were used to the idea of having to buy their way in. This offer was different. It would take a "change of mind" about God and how He operates. They would have to enter the kingdom of their loving, powerful, and holy Creator by faith . . . apart from works.

There are forces at work in the world today that still try to "arrest" the voices crying in the wilderness. Much is being done to squelch the message that God offers forgiveness by grace alone, apart from works (Ephesians 2:8–9). Let's not allow these forces to keep this message from getting through.

As a result of the truth in these two verses in Mark, consider several things:

—never let your voice be silenced when sharing the truth about the grace of God;

—be as available to people who need this message as Jesus was, and;

—remember where your citizenship is (in the Kingdom of God, not man) and then live like it.

What a difference we could make in the world if we could consistently do those three things!

Life Interrupted

As He was going along by the Sea of Galilee, He saw
Simon and Andrew, the brother of Simon, casting a net in
the sea; for they were fishermen. And Jesus said to them,
"Follow Me, and I will make you become fishers of men."
Immediately they left their nets and followed Him. Going
on a little farther, He saw James the son of Zebedee, and
John his brother, who were also in the boat mending the
nets. Immediately He called them; and they left their
father Zebedee in the boat with the hired servants, and
went away to follow Him.

MARK 1:16–20

IN HIS PURSUIT of his wayward creation, Jesus walks into the life
of some men who think they are living ... but aren't. They would
soon find out that there is a huge difference between eking out a
living and truly living. Jesus interrupted lives that were very small
compared to what they one day would become.

Only God can show us the proper vision for our lives. Only
God can walk into the small existence we call life, the life we desperately hold onto, and show us that it is okay to loosen our grip
enough to make a trade.

Two sets of brothers, Simon and Andrew, and James and John,
may have thought fishing for fish was all they would be able to
look forward to the rest of their lives. They may have settled into
those small lives not knowing God desired to interrupt them with
something much bigger. To those who were casting nets day in and
day out, Jesus cast a vision for eternity by saying, "Follow me, and I
will make you become fishers of men" (Mark 1:17). He was offering them a chance to be a significant force in the kingdom of God.
Rather than pulling fish from the sea in order for people to live
physical lives, He offered them a chance to pull people from the

darkness of sin and its effects in order to live forever. When you start talking about a life that impacts eternity, you are talking about a very big life!

These bigger lives all started when they put down their nets and started following the One who interrupted. Let's let God interrupt our lives with His vision for us. He is pursuing us even now. A loose grip on small lives sets the stage for the great exchange ... small lives for big ones!

A Liberating Force

They went into Capernaum; and immediately on the
Sabbath He entered the synagogue and [began] to teach.
They were amazed at His teaching; for He was teaching
them as [one] having authority, and not as the scribes. Just
then there was a man in their synagogue with an unclean
spirit; and he cried out, saying, "What business do we have
with each other, Jesus of Nazareth? Have You come to
destroy us? I know who You are—the Holy One of God!"
And Jesus rebuked him, saying, "Be quiet, and come out of
him!" Throwing him into convulsions, the unclean spirit
cried out with a loud voice and came out of him. They
were all amazed, so that they debated among themselves,
saying, "What is this? A new teaching with authority! He
commands even the unclean spirits, and they obey Him."
Immediately the news about Him spread everywhere into
all the surrounding district of Galilee.

MARK 1:21–28

As you know, the struggle to liberate Iraq was not without a fight.
The old regime had to give up a lot of territory, but again, it was not
without a fight.

In reading this account of Jesus in the synagogue, you realize the
spiritual enemy had to give up some vital territory, but not without
a fight of his own. Once Jesus had begun to gather a small squad
of warriors (the first four disciples) He immediately established
a "beachhead." The invading forces landed in a synagogue where
people had apparently grown used to hearing lifeless teaching from
scribes who approached the Scriptures as more of a textbook than
the living Word of God.

Jesus was not only able to establish His authority in the life of
that small synagogue but He was able to establish His authority in

the life of a single man who was in the grip of an "occupying force." Jesus' words and works put everyone in Galilee on notice that a liberating force had arrived. The Living Word of God was in town.

I hope you can realize the significance of this for you and me. Jesus, the Living Word of God, has come into hostile territory to reveal the heart of God in such away that we would be blown away by its power and authority. I hope you can realize the opportunity we have every time we open the Scriptures. Truth and light filling our minds and hearts to the point where life makes sense and our hearts respond to the living Word rather than a lifeless textbook.

Keep in mind the life of that one man liberated by Jesus that day. That same freedom is offered to you and me. Allow God to free you from whatever it is that has captured your heart … whether anger, sadness, uncertainty, lust, fear, bitterness, or loneliness.

Keep in mind that the liberating force has arrived. Let's stand on the streets and sidewalks waving and welcoming Him into our daily lives. There is much more territory to be taken, you know. There are many more lives in need of the Living Word of God. I have it on good authority that He is looking to recruit some more warriors. Any volunteers?

Doors Wide Open

And immediately after they came out of the synagogue, they came into the house of Simon and Andrew, with James and John. Now Simon's mother-in-law was lying sick with a fever; and immediately they spoke to Jesus about her. And He came to her and raised her up, taking her by the hand, and the fever left her, and she waited on them.

When evening came, after the sun had set, they [began] bringing to Him all who were ill and those who were demon-possessed. And the whole city had gathered at the door. And He healed many who were ill with various diseases, and cast out many demons; and He was not permitting the demons to speak, because they knew who He was.

MARK 1:29–34

WE ARE SEEING an important progression as we watch the life of Christ revealed in this first chapter of Mark. Jesus touches the life of one man in a synagogue then the life of a family in a home and then the life of "the whole city."

The man in the synagogue was impacted by the words of Christ while Simon's mother-in-law was impacted by the touch of Christ. What we see in the progression is His influence, His saving grace, and His healing power reaching a whole city.

The Scriptures are honest in telling us that Jesus had the desire and the power to heal many who were sick with various diseases. "The whole city" was at the door and the door was wide open—how else could they all get in to be with Jesus?

Many of us have experienced the power of both Jesus' words and touch in our lives. We know what it is to see His impact on our families. It is now time to throw the front door wide open and allow "the whole city" to experience the same.

I believe God will use His Church to do just that. He has called us to get the word out about who He is and what He wants to do in the lives of individuals, families, cities, and even the world. Notice in this passage that Jesus would not allow the demons to speak because they knew who He was. Since the demons aren't allowed to get the word out, guess who gets that great privilege and duty? You are exactly right . . . you and I!

While we may be used to keeping the doors of our homes shut and locked tight for safety's sake, let's keep in mind the tremendous need to keep the church doors wide open. There is a whole city needing to experience the words and touch of Christ.

A Dark and Secluded Place

In the early morning, while it was still dark, Jesus got up, left [the house], and went away to a secluded place, and was praying there. Simon and his companions searched for Him; they found Him, and said to Him, "Everyone is looking for You." He said to them, "Let us go somewhere else to the towns nearby, so that I may preach there also; for that is what I came for." And He went into their synagogues throughout all Galilee, preaching and casting out the demons.

MARK 1:35–39

❦

JESUS LEFT THE house and went away to a dark and secluded place ... but He was not alone. He went out to talk and listen to His Father. Because alone time with His Father was a priority in His life, Jesus sacrificed that extra hour of sleep. We are not told *what* He prayed but we are told *that* He prayed.

There was a tremendous amount of work for Jesus to do. He came to save the world, you know. Should He not get going? If we pay close attention, we will notice the "going" came after the "being." Being with the Father was just as much a part of His mission as going "somewhere else to towns nearby" (Mark 1:38).

Simon's words to Him were, "Everyone is looking for you." No pressure, right? It seems the whole world was in pain at that very moment and everyone was searching for the One with all the power. And where did they find Him? Alone with His Father. Jesus knew how important it was to give His Father first place among "everyone."

The hard question you and I must answer is whether we have learned that lesson ourselves. There was a lot of activity in Jesus' life just as there is in ours. There is a tremendous amount of going and coming for us as we function in our well lit homes and offices.

There is very little seclusion for us in our crowded lives. We get very used to doing lots of things, especially for God. Many of us don't sit down and rest much because we can still hear our fathers saying, "Don't just stand there, do something!"

There is a dark and secluded place for all of us in which to be alone with the Father. To avoid the alone time and to jump straight into the work at hand is a huge mistake.

Let me ask you this . . . what good are you and I to "everyone" if we have not been alone with "the One"?

A Willing Touch

And a leper came to Jesus, beseeching Him and falling
on his knees before Him, and saying, "If You are willing,
You can make me clean." Moved with compassion, Jesus
stretched out His hand and touched him, and said to him,
"I am willing; be cleansed." Immediately the leprosy left
him and he was cleansed. And He sternly warned him
and immediately sent him away, and He said to him, "See
that you say nothing to anyone; but go, show yourself
to the priest and offer for your cleansing what Moses
commanded, as a testimony to them." But he went out and
began to proclaim it freely and to spread the news around,
to such an extent that Jesus could no longer publicly enter
a city, but stayed out in unpopulated areas; and they were
coming to Him from everywhere.

MARK 1:40–45

⸎

IT HAD NEVER been done before. No one had ever willingly touched
a leper, much less healed one. It was a terrible disease that affected
a person's nerve endings. This means lepers would unwittingly do
terrible damage to their bodies because they could not feel pain.
The infections that would develop caused body parts to rot which
led to horrible disfigurement. The sight and smell of leprosy was
extremely offensive. It was a disease that had no cure and it was a
disease that had no hope . . . until Jesus came along.

The only thing society knew to do with lepers was to separate
them into their own communities. Lepers were forced to cover
themselves completely if they were to enter a town. They were required to stay far away from those who were healthy and forced to
announce their affliction in a loud voice. *Leper! Leper!* This humili-
ating proclamation would give people enough warning so that the
leper could be avoided.

There's really no telling how long this man had gone without a willing touch from a loving human being. He did, however, know enough about Jesus to know that He *could* heal him. His question was about something else. *Are You willing?* Jesus surprised all those who were watching by reaching out His hand and revealing His heart. "Of course, I am willing," Jesus said as He placed His healing hand on the man's rotting body.

To be rejected by people is one thing. But what about God? How does He feel about us? Our sin is as offensive to God as the sights and smells of leprosy would be to you and me. Sin separates people from their loving Creator and causes spiritual death which leads to another kind of rot. Do you believe that God is able and willing to touch your life in such a way as to take away the rot of sin?

I am praying that you will know the willing and powerful touch of God on your life. He is not only *able* to make a difference, but He is *willing* to make a difference. What would you like for Jesus to touch in your life? I want you to know that what He did for that leprous man on the dusty streets of Galilee two thousand years ago, He is willing to do for you today, right where you are.

Speaking of where you are ... did you notice all of this happened to the leper as he *knelt* at the feet of Christ? Think about it!

Our Greatest Need

When He had come back to Capernaum several days
afterward, it was heard that He was at home. And many
were gathered together, so that there was no longer room,
not even near the door; and He was speaking the word to
them. And they came, bringing to Him a paralytic, carried
by four men. Being unable to get to Him because of the
crowd, they removed the roof above Him; and when they
had dug an opening, they let down the pallet on which
the paralytic was lying. And Jesus seeing their faith said
to the paralytic, "Son, your sins are forgiven." But some of
the scribes were sitting there and reasoning in their hearts,
"Why does this man speak that way? He is blaspheming;
who can forgive sins but God alone?" Immediately Jesus,
aware in His spirit that they were reasoning that way
within themselves, said to them, "Why are you reasoning
about these things in your hearts? "Which is easier, to
say to the paralytic, 'Your sins are forgiven'; or to say, 'Get
up, and pick up your pallet and walk'? But so that you
may know that the Son of Man has authority on earth
to forgive sins"—He said to the paralytic, "I say to you,
get up, pick up your pallet and go home." And he got up
and immediately picked up the pallet and went out in the
sight of everyone, so that they were all amazed and were
glorifying God, saying, "We have never seen anything like
this."

And He went out again by the seashore; and all the
people were coming to Him, and He was teaching them.

MARK 2:1–13

❧

THIS YOUNG MAN was fortunate to have four friends who did not
mind carrying him around. This young man was fortunate to have

four friends who cared about his greatest need. The four men who carried the stretcher believed, as the young man probably did at that time, that his greatest need in life was to be able to walk. But were they right?

Word had gotten out that Jesus had power to heal and so the four friends carried their paralyzed buddy to Jesus. After a great deal of effort to get their friend past the crowd, through the front door and in front of Jesus, they finally realized they had to move to "Plan B." I don't know about you, but I am very familiar with "Plan B." Failure has put me on to "Plan B" many times.

After quite a bit of damage to the roof, along with some good old-fashioned teamwork and a touch of engineering, the young man was in front of Jesus, ready to receive his new legs. Right? Not so fast! It was at this point that everyone learned what the real need in his life was . . . forgiveness.

Carrying the burden and weight of a paralyzed friend is no comparison to carrying the weight of our own paralyzed heart. A heart paralyzed by sin and all that sin produces—things such as fear, anger, hatred, lust, bitterness, resentment, pain, or sadness—hangs in a person's chest as heavy and useless as an iron bell with no clapper.

No doubt we have all thought, at one time or another, that our greatest need in life was more money, a nicer car, a bigger house, a better job, a thinner body, better kids, or even a healthier self im-age. I hope we can change our minds about this. Our greatest need is to receive forgiveness from our Heavenly Father. Only then does life move on.

Allow Christ to meet that need today. Find yourself at His feet, hearing those healing words, "My son, your sins are forgiven." Don't let the crowd keep you away any longer. Our heart is like a heavy and useless bell inside our chest until a clapper (life) is installed.

That young man actually got new legs that day, but only after he got a new heart through forgiveness. I wonder, as he *walked* out of that house that day, if somewhere in town a bell was ringing, as if to announce that a life had started over. Just a thought.

The Doctor is In

As He passed by, He saw Levi the [son] of Alphaeus
sitting in the tax booth, and He said to him, "Follow Me!"
And he got up and followed Him.

And it happened that He was reclining [at the table] in
his house, and many tax collectors and sinners were dining
with Jesus and His disciples; for there were many of them,
and they were following Him. When the scribes of the
Pharisees saw that He was eating with the sinners and tax
collectors, they said to His disciples, "Why is He eating
and drinking with tax collectors and sinners?" And hearing
[this], Jesus said to them, "[It is] not those who are healthy
who need a physician, but those who are sick; I did not
come to call the righteous, but sinners."

MARK 2:14–17

CONFINED TO A very small booth as he collected both the poll tax (a
tax on income) and ground tax (a tax on property), Matthew lived
a most miserable life. Not only was he miserable but he was actively
contributing to the misery of others. As a tax collector he was a
puppet of the Roman Empire and was hated by the Palestinians
of that day. Because of this, he was very alone in that very small
booth.

By inviting Matthew to follow, Jesus took him from the sick and
confining life of a tax collector, to the healthy and expansive life
found only in Christ, the Great Physician. Because of the new life
he found in following Jesus, Matthew threw a dinner party for all
his unsavory friends and associates. And there at the table eating
and drinking with these ruffians were Jesus and His friends.

Matthew may have been giving himself a going away party since
he was leaving that old way of life. Whatever the reason for the
dinner party, the religious crowd was not pleased. Jesus was "eating

and drinking" with sinners and tax collectors. The religious establishment was up in arms over this and had some hard questions for Jesus and His friends. That is when Jesus explained a little more about the mission He was on.

You see, it is like a doctor who actually *touches* sick people! (Caution! Continue reading at your own risk.)

Just as Jesus befriended sinners and tax collectors, you and I are to befriend unbelievers. It is obviously easier to surround ourselves with like-minded folks. Having only Christian friends is a much more convenient way to live life. But God did not command us to live convenient lives. He commanded us to take the message of the Great Physician into a very sick and depraved world. To do that, we will have to actually *touch* the lives of people who hate us.

If we as believers isolate ourselves from our neighbors whose lives are shattered by the same sin that once shattered ours, and if we never reach out with the truth about the healing and forgiving power of the Great Physician, then we may need to take the "Jesus fish" off the back of our cars so people won't mistake us for hypocrites. If you and I do not readily have a number of non-Christian friends that we are actively loving and to whom we are communicating the truth of the gospel and praying for, then we have not yet caught the vision of Jesus Himself.

There are people all around us whose lives are confined by the disease of sin. Let's starting throwing a few more "going away parties" and see if we can't get some of these unsavory friends and associates of ours to "go away" with us.

Relationship Rather Than Religion

John's disciples and the Pharisees were fasting; and they came and said to Him, "Why do John's disciples and the disciples of the Pharisees fast, but Your disciples do not fast?" And Jesus said to them, "While the bridegroom is with them, the attendants of the bridegroom cannot fast, can they? So long as they have the bridegroom with them, they cannot fast. But the days will come when the bridegroom is taken away from them, and then they will fast in that day.

"No one sews a patch of unshrunk cloth on an old garment; otherwise the patch pulls away from it, the new from the old, and a worse tear results. No one puts new wine into old wineskins; otherwise the wine will burst the skins, and the wine is lost and the skins [as well]; but [one puts] new wine into fresh wineskins."

MARK 2:18–22

FASTING IS ONE of the great spiritual disciplines of the faith. It is to be a vital part of our spiritual journey and it can be just that if we do not spoil it with religion. By religion I simply mean a dry lifeless duty by which we try to reach God on our own terms. It has been said that religion is man's attempt to reach God, while the Christian faith is God's attempt to reach man. Jesus came to show us the difference between a religion and a relationship. He came to shake things up and He certainly did that when He and His friends refused to fast along with the others.

Notice that Jesus answered the Pharisees' concerns about His failure to fast with a great word picture that revolves around the celebration of relationships. There is a time to fast and a time to feast and Jesus is showing them the difference.

We feast in celebration of the loving relationship and commitment between a bride and groom. All eyes are on those two beautiful people as we celebrate their love with tears in our eyes. Along with that, the groom and his groomsmen are doing nothing but celebrating—celebrating the passage of a young man into manhood as the groom takes that huge step of commitment born of love.

Jesus was telling them then and is telling us today that life with God is not about religion but about relationship. It was a new day in Galilee as the God of the universe arrived to call men and women into a personal relationship. As if to say, *Let go of the old way of thinking. Let go of the old way of approaching God.* He is not interested in our attempts to reach Him because He knows our work is not good enough. The question is whether we know that.

New cloth sewed to old cloth is a disaster. New wine in cracked wine skins is not only a disaster but it creates quite a mess. Man trying to reach God with his good works is not only a disaster but it leaves life broken and messy. God desires for us to be in a personal relationship with Him. He desires a relationship that takes us to the banquet table of feasting and celebrating.

There will come a very sad day when the groomsmen will become pallbearers. Fasting will fit very well on that day. Grief will rob them of their appetites. But until that day, the groomsmen are to feast in celebration of their relationship with the groom. The same is true for us. God has called us into a relationship rather than a religion and we need to celebrate that with a feast. Don't get me wrong, there is certainly a place for fasting in our spiritual journey. Let's just be careful we don't forget that there is a time and place for everything.

Remember, there are two beautiful people on the dance floor right now and one of them is you. I say we have something to celebrate!

Sabbath Lessons

And it happened that He was passing through the
grainfields on the Sabbath, and His disciples began to
make their way along while picking the heads [of grain].
The Pharisees were saying to Him, "Look, why are they
doing what is not lawful on the Sabbath?" And He said to
them, "Have you never read what David did when he was
in need and he and his companions became hungry; how
he entered the house of God in the time of Abiathar [the]
high priest, and ate the consecrated bread, which is not
lawful for [anyone] to eat except the priests, and he also
gave it to those who were with him?" Jesus said to them,
"The Sabbath was made for man, and not man for the
Sabbath. So the Son of Man is Lord even of the Sabbath."

MARK 2:23–28

A SIMPLE WALK with the Lord through the grainfields of Galilee
erupted into quite a controversy. It seems Jesus' friends crossed over
one of the Pharisees' proverbial lines. I am sure it came as a shock
to the disciples when they found out a line had been crossed, but
with the Pharisees, crossing the line was easy.

I can imagine the Pharisees would have blown an ear-pierc-
ing whistle, passionately raising one hand in the air and screaming, "Foul!" had the opportunity been afforded them. These religious thugs did what came naturally to them, they complained
about something they knew very little about—the purpose of the
Sabbath.

The Pharisees were good at building restrictive boundaries
around good things. They took legitimate laws handed down by
God for the provision and protection of His people and turned
them into burdensome rules that sucked the life out of God's chosen ones. The mandate to keep the Sabbath holy became so dis-

torted that someone could be in violation by simply picking a long piece of grass and chewing on it while walking. That sort of thing bothered Jesus so much, I am sure He was ready to stand up with His own whistle and call out, "Foul!"

The foul was simple. God gave the Sabbath to man as a provision for his rest and recovery. A day to worship rather than a day to hustle was—and is—very much needed for creatures like you and me who are driven to conquer and succeed. The Sabbath was given to man as if God were saying, "Rest My little warriors. Rest today for I assure you the battle will still be there tomorrow. You can continue the fight—after your nap."

Pulling back from our work is important to God. He even modeled it for us. Not because *He* needed a break but because He knew *we* would need one. He showed us how it is done. Jesus identified Himself as "the Lord of the Sabbath." He was letting them know that it was He who made the law which provided a time of rest and spiritual focus. Jesus was not about to let a group of religious hooligans spoil a good thing.

So let me encourage you to do something. Take a walk with the Lord through a field (if only in your imagination). Break off a long piece of grass and chew on it as you walk. Look Jesus in the eye and make a commitment to take one day a week just to rest and reflect. And when you are rested, see if you can't hear Christ say to you, *Go back to the battle my little warrior. Go back to the fight!*

Out In The Open

He entered again into a synagogue; and a man was there whose hand was withered. They were watching Him [to see] if He would heal him on the Sabbath, so that they might accuse Him. He said to the man with the withered hand, "Get up and come forward!" And He said to them, "Is it lawful to do good or to do harm on the Sabbath, to save a life or to kill?" But they kept silent. After looking around at them with anger, grieved at their hardness of heart, He said to the man, "Stretch out your hand." And he stretched it out, and his hand was restored. The Pharisees went out and immediately [began] conspiring with the Herodians against Him, [as] [to] how they might destroy Him.

MARK 3:1–6

IN A PLACE where people should have welcomed Jesus with open arms, He found closed and hardened hearts. In a place where people should have had the freedom to reveal their imperfect lives, Jesus found a man who may have learned to hide his.

Still angry over the now infamous "grainfield incident," the Pharisees continued to watch Jesus closely to see if He would do anything worth an accusation. All the while, a man with a deformed and imperfect hand stood in their midst. I have wondered for some time what, if any, technique the man used to cover up his deformity. I am sure years of schoolyard teasing and public staring sent him looking for the best way to conceal his withered hand. *Maybe I could have my mom sew one sleeve longer than the other. Perhaps if I keep my hand in my pocket or if I walk with my hand behind my back, fewer people will notice. Perhaps if I cross my arms with my hand tucked away I could avoid the staring.* I am sure all these were options if he wanted to avoid the humiliation.

I wonder how scared the man was when Jesus called him to the front. How scared do you think he was to be asked to stand in front of Jesus and all those religious people? It is not out of the realm of possibility to think the Pharisees would quote the Scripture that says, "... the sins of the fathers will be visited upon the children." Wouldn't it be the religious ruffians who would tell him that his deformity was a result of his sin or his parent's sin? That's what some religious people told my father about his cleft palate. I don't believe he ever got over that shame. I am not sure he ever fully recovered from the damage done by that message.

For the man in this passage, it took a courageous act of faith to stretch out his hand to Jesus. To stretch his hand out meant it had to come out into the open for everyone to see. That was the bad news. The good news was this—there was *restoration* once the hand was brought out into the open, once the hand was *given* to Jesus. Jesus' healing power overtook the deformed hand and returned it to its original design.

There are many things in our lives that can remind us of that withered hand—hidden away in fear. Struggling marriages can be like that. Addictions that pull us down can be like that as well. We work alongside people everyday whose lives are obviously not what they were designed to be. You and I have been hurt by religious people who work to tear down rather than restore damaged lives. Let's not be like that.

If there is something you are hiding from God and from others out of fear, let me encourage you to bring it out into the open. Only then does the restoring power of Christ overtake that which is damaged. Marriages, addictions, fears, and shame are all redeemable. Let's let go of the techniques we have developed to hide our withered lives. Let's bring them out into the open where they can be overtaken by the grace and power of God.

Crushing Crowds

Jesus withdrew to the sea with His disciples; and a great
multitude from Galilee followed; and [also] from Judea,
and from Jerusalem, and from Idumea, and beyond the
Jordan, and the vicinity of Tyre and Sidon, a great number
of people heard of all that He was doing and came to Him.
And He told His disciples that a boat should stand ready
for Him because of the crowd, so that they would not
crowd Him; for He had healed many, with the result that
all those who had afflictions pressed around Him in order
to touch Him. Whenever the unclean spirits saw Him,
they would fall down before Him and shout, "You are the
Son of God!" And He earnestly warned them not to tell
who He was.

MARK 3:7–12

❧

IF YOU HAVE ever tossed a rock into the calm water of a lake, you
have had the experience of seeing concentric ripples expand outward, creating circles that eventually fade away. Word about Jesus
hit Galilee like a rock and the ripples expanded outward to such
a degree that thousands of people eventually formed a crushing
crowd around Him.

If you look at a map of Israel as it was in the time of Christ,
you will see that Galilee was "Ground Zero" and Jesus' impact was
reaching outward:

—through Jerusalem to the south, Judea even more to the south,
and Idumea which was Israel's most southern border;

—"beyond the Jordan" which is to the east;

—through the Tyre and Sidon region which is northwest of
Galilee.

The Rock hit in Galilee and the ripples went out from there.

Crushing crowds of the afflicted pushed Jesus to the water's edge as they sought His loving and powerful touch. They sought Him out because word about Him had gotten out.

Those crowds have not diminished one bit today. Walk through a shopping mall at Christmas time or go to your nearest theater megaplex and you will get an idea of the kind of crowd needing Jesus' grace and power. It would not be hard for us to see the crowd as an inconvenience—but I hope we won't see it that way. Crushing crowds are not an inconvenience when we see them through the eyes of Jesus. They are afflicted individuals in desperate need of a Savior.

I cannot think of a better word to describe the misery we see and feel around us other than *affliction*. It is a condition of great physical, mental, and spiritual distress. The world around us (our friends and families) are in this kind of distress. Who will tell them about Jesus? Who will identify Him as *The Rock*?

It is clear in today's passage that the evil spirits were not (and are not) allowed to reveal Jesus' identity. That means it is up to you and me. Toss a rock on a calm lake and the ripples move out in concentric circles until they eventually fade away. Tell a person the truth about Jesus and the ripples move out for eternity, never fading away.

Summoned and Appointed

And He went up on the mountain and summoned those whom He Himself wanted, and they came to Him. And He appointed twelve, so that they would be with Him and that He [could] send them out to preach, and to have authority to cast out the demons. And He appointed the twelve: Simon (to whom He gave the name Peter), and James, the [son] of Zebedee, and John the brother of James (to them He gave the name Boanerges, which means, "Sons of Thunder"); and Andrew, and Philip, and Bartholomew, and Matthew, and Thomas, and James the son of Alphaeus, and Thaddaeus, and Simon the Zealot; and Judas Iscariot, who betrayed Him.

MARK 3:13–19

As I READ about Jesus' selection of His twelve disciples, I was struck by two very important words: summoned and appointed. To be called into a close circle of friendship with Jesus at a point when crushing crowds were becoming an everyday occurrence must have communicated a certain amount of confidence and value. To hear something from Jesus along the lines of, *From out of the throngs of individuals, I choose you!* must have communicated love.

Jesus, I assure you, did not do this to *exclude* anyone from within the crowd. On the contrary, He did this to *reach* the crowd. The throngs, the crowds, the masses, the cities, the nations, the world were all so dear to Him that He summoned a dozen individuals with a plan to empower them to reach the many. Jesus called these guys from out of the crowd and into a loving relationship in order to reach the crowds that were in desperate need of that same kind of relationship with God.

Once summoned, those dear friends of Jesus were appointed. The assignment would be an impossible one if they tried to do it apart from Christ. They were appointed and assigned to share the Good News and thus free people from spiritual death. They were joining in on what Jesus was already doing.

Can you remember that moment in your life when you were summoned by the Son of God? Can you remember what it felt like to be noticed by Him in the midst of all humanity and to hear your name spoken? Remember—you and I were not called out of the crowd just to make our lives easy. We were summoned for an appointment. You and I were called out of the crowd in order to be empowered to go right back in with a message. That is *not* an easy assignment. It is actually impossible if we attempt it apart from Christ.

You and I have been called into a loving relationship with God. It is a relationship that has brought us out of death and into life. Let's remember that there is a huge crowd still needing us to go back in with two things: the truth about what life is meant to be in Christ and the freedom found in Him. There are many more within the crowd who are waiting to hear Christ whisper something like, *From out of the throngs of individuals, I choose you!* Surely the Lord will give you an opportunity to pass that message on to someone today. Surely!

A Line In The Sand

And He came home, and the crowd gathered again, to
such an extent that they could not even eat a meal. When
His own people heard [of] [this], they went out to take
custody of Him; for they were saying, "He has lost His
senses." The scribes who came down from Jerusalem were
saying, "He is possessed by Beelzebul," and "He casts out
the demons by the ruler of the demons." And He called
them to Himself and began speaking to them in parables,
"How can Satan cast out Satan? If a kingdom is divided
against itself, that kingdom cannot stand. If a house is
divided against itself, that house will not be able to stand.
If Satan has risen up against himself and is divided, he
cannot stand, but he is finished! But no one can enter the
strong man's house and plunder his property unless he first
binds the strong man, and then he will plunder his house.

"Truly I say to you, all sins shall be forgiven the sons
of men, and whatever blasphemies they utter; but whoever
blasphemes against the Holy Spirit never has forgiveness,
but is guilty of an eternal sin"—because they were saying,
"He has an unclean spirit."

MARK 3:20–30

❧

THE SACRIFICE OF discipleship (following Jesus) must have become
more and more clear to His friends as the crowds continued to
swell. The needs of the many individuals who were ready to lay
their lives before Jesus were necessarily coming before their own
needs. They were hungry but they could not eat a meal.

The sacrifices were not just physical. I believe the sacrifices
showed up in the pain caused by the accusations, doubts, and mis-
understandings of some of those in the crowd. Religious leaders
and family members did not believe Jesus was who He said He was.

So Jesus drew a line in the sand, so to speak. *Either you believe that I am God and live forever or you believe that I am Satan and never know forgiveness.*

Jesus drew the line in the sand right then and there. It will all come down to what you and I believe about Jesus. To believe He was empowered by Satan to mislead us is to reject Him. To believe that He was the Son of God empowered by the Holy Spirit is to understand and receive the Truth.

Notice that He gave a glimpse into His mission—enter the strong man's house, tie him up, and plunder. He came to retrieve that which was (and is) rightfully His—you and me.

Too many people fail to elevate Jesus, the Mighty Plunderer, to His proper place in their lives. To see Him as merely a legitimate option on the buffet of world religious leaders is to see Him as merely "a cut above" the rest of human beings rather than the Creator of human beings.

So you tell me, did Jesus lie about who He was? Did He know He was just a man and thus lie when He said He was God? Had Jesus really lost His senses? Was He crazy in that He *thought* He was God but really wasn't? C.S. Lewis argued that Jesus was either a *liar*, a *lunatic*, or *Lord*.

Jesus' family (for a while) saw Him as a lunatic and were saying *Lock Him away.*

The scribes saw Him as a liar and were saying *Look past Him for the truth.*

Many in the crowd saw Him as Lord and were saying *Lay down your life.*

You and I are not lost in the crowd. We are individuals created by God for God. We must decide what we believe about Him. If Jesus was a *lunatic*, then we must keep our distance as well as warn others to do the same. If Jesus was a *liar*, then we must stop calling Him a "good teacher" since He cannot be trusted. If He is *Lord*, then we must submit our lives to Him. Talk about the sacrifice of discipleship . . .

Family of God

Then His mother and His brothers arrived, and standing outside they sent [word] to Him and called Him. A crowd was sitting around Him, and they said to Him, "Behold, Your mother and Your brothers are outside looking for You." Answering them, He said, "Who are My mother and My brothers?" Looking about at those who were sitting around Him, He said, "Behold My mother and My brothers! For whoever does the will of God, he is My brother and sister and mother."

MARK 3:31–35

TODAY'S PASSAGE FOCUSES on what it is to be in Jesus' family. There is a great deal we can learn in our earthly families. There is even more we can learn in Jesus' family. The family is a creation of God and designed to be a place of support and encouragement. It is to be a place of love and learning. The family is a place of leadership and discipleship. The family is where we learn to share, care, do chores, love, communicate, flex, follow the leader, pitch in, pray and learn to fight fairly. The family, in its purest and healthiest form, is a gift from God.

In today's passage, Jesus' mother and brothers (His physical family) were looking for Him. We learned in an earlier passage that they had some real concerns about Him. We learned that they felt He had lost His senses. They were trying to decide if He was a *liar*, a *lunatic*, or if He was truly the *Lord*. Had they come to take Him away to a safe place? Were they looking to protect Him from Himself and/or from others? Whatever their reason, we learn an important lesson about family life with Jesus.

What is it to be rightly related to Jesus? What is it to be in a family with Him? According to Jesus, to do the will of God is to be in the family of God. Jesus said, "Behold My mother and My brothers! For whoever does the will of God, he is My brother and sister and mother" (Mark 3:34–35). The "will of God" is not spelled out in a definitive list anywhere in this passage. Jesus did not list the *dos* and *don'ts* of the Christian faith and family. Jesus simply defined the family of God as those who do the will of God. When asked about the "works of God," Jesus said, "This is the work of God, that you believe in Him whom He has sent" (John 6:28).

You and I are a part of our physical families because of our physical birth. Our physical birth put us in our earthly families. The same is true about our spiritual family. Our spiritual birth through faith put us in our spiritual family. The process of growing up started on our birthday. If done according to God's design, our physical families are a safe place to grow and learn. If done according to God's design, our spiritual family is a safe place to grow and learn as well.

Jesus was able to say on that day something like, *Look, here are true spiritual family members. Their birthday was the day they believed in Me. They know I am not a liar or a lunatic.* Our place in God's family is secured by God's power and grace. His family is a safe place to learn how to share and care as well as to do chores. It is a place to love, communicate, flex, and follow the leader. It is where we learn to pitch in as well as pray. It is where we learn to fight fairly. The family, in its purest and healthiest form, is a gift from God. To be in God's family *is* pure and healthy. Enjoy!

Gift-Wrapped Truth

He began to teach again by the sea. And such a very large crowd gathered to Him that He got into a boat in the sea and sat down; and the whole crowd was by the sea on the land. And He was teaching them many things in parables, and was saying to them in His teaching, "Listen [to this]! Behold, the sower went out to sow; as he was sowing, some [seed] fell beside the road, and the birds came and ate it up. Other [seed] fell on the rocky [ground] where it did not have much soil; and immediately it sprang up because it had no depth of soil. And after the sun had risen, it was scorched; and because it had no root, it withered away. Other [seed] fell among the thorns, and the thorns came up and choked it, and it yielded no crop. Other [seeds] fell into the good soil, and as they grew up and increased, they yielded a crop and produced thirty, sixty, and a hundredfold." And He was saying, "He who has ears to hear, let him hear."

As soon as He was alone, His followers, along with the twelve, [began] asking Him [about] the parables. And He was saying to them, "To you has been given the mystery of the kingdom of God, but those who are outside get everything in parables, so that WHILE SEEING, THEY MAY SEE AND NOT PERCEIVE, AND WHILE HEARING, THEY MAY HEAR AND NOT UNDERSTAND, OTHERWISE THEY MIGHT RETURN AND BE FORGIVEN."

MARK 4:1–12

⬥

ONCE THE LINE had been drawn in the sand, so to speak (either people believed Jesus was Lord or they didn't), Jesus began teaching the large crowds in parables. There were two main reasons for us- ing parables. Within the crowd, there were those who remained on the other side of the line, those who *did not* believe in Him. These were folks who had ears but would not hear. They did not believe the truth that had been revealed so they would now hear new truth in a veiled way, wrapped in a parable. On the other side of the line were those who *did* believe in Him. These were folks who had "ears to hear" and so new truth would be revealed to them. Parables were not used to keep people from believing the truth: they were used to veil new truth to those who refused to believe the truth already given.

Notice in this passage that Jesus continued to provide truth to the masses. He positioned Himself in a way that allowed everyone to physically hear the message. He took the time to get in a boat and push out just enough to project life-saving and life-giving truth into the crowd. While the majority could *physically* hear Him, there is no doubt many would not *spiritually* hear Him. They chose not to. For them the truth would now be wrapped in a parable. If and when they put their faith in Him, all would change—the new truth would make sense as they received and unwrapped the gift.

Before we unwrap our Christmas or birthday presents, there is a great mystery. *What could this be? I hope it is just what I wanted.* All one must do to solve the mystery is simply unwrap the gift. Take the paper off and there it is, the gift chosen and purchased just for you. No more mystery.

This is how it was for those who received the truth given by Jesus. "To you has been given the mystery of the kingdom of God, but those who are outside get everything in parables ... " (Mark 4:11). The outsiders lose out. They reject the truth given plainly and will now have to hear new truth veiled. All they would need to do to understand the mystery of the kingdom of God is to come in from the outside. Faith is the key to this journey. Faith takes someone from one side of the line to the other, from outside to inside.

On one side of the line, one hears of the seed, the sower, and the soils and is encouraged. On the other side of the line, one hears of the same things and is confused. One person receives the truth wrapped in a parable and leaves it wrapped. One person receives the mystery of the kingdom of God, unwraps it with faith and screams, *Wow! Just what I always wanted! Just what I always needed!* Which one are you? What will you do with the gift-wrapped truth?

The Soil Of Our Hearts

And He said to them, "Do you not understand this parable? How will you understand all the parables? The sower sows the word. These are the ones who are beside the road where the word is sown; and when they hear, immediately Satan comes and takes away the word which has been sown in them. In a similar way these are the ones on whom seed was sown on the rocky [places], who, when they hear the word, immediately receive it with joy; and they have no [firm] root in themselves, but are [only] temporary; then, when affliction or persecution arises because of the word, immediately they fall away. And others are the ones on whom seed was sown among the thorns; these are the ones who have heard the word, but the worries of the world, and the deceitfulness of riches, and the desires for other things enter in and choke the word, and it becomes unfruitful. And those are the ones on whom seed was sown on the good soil; and they hear the word and accept it and bear fruit, thirty, sixty, and a hundredfold."

MARK 4:13–20

HEART DISEASE IS one of the leading causes of death in the United States. The medical community is desperately trying to get the message out that the condition of a person's heart matters in life. If the heart is healthy then life is prolonged and enjoyed. Millions of dollars are invested in research and treatment of heart disease because the condition of the heart matters.

Just as the condition of the heart matters in life, the condition of soil matters in farming. A tremendous amount of money and effort goes into preparing the soil for planting. Farmers prepare the soil before sowing the seed. Jesus described four kinds of soil in His parable that were visuals for understanding four kinds of conditions of a person's spiritual heart. Jesus described a soil that is hard-packed, a soil that is rocky, a soil that is thorny, and soil that is good. One of these soils, I believe, describes a person who never receives the truth of God's Word and thus never comes alive spiritually. The other three describe those believers who have received the Word and need to give attention to the condition of the "soil" of their hearts.

Farmers know that hard-packed dirt does not receive the seed. The seed sits on top of the ground, never going into it. That seed becomes bird food. Farmers also know the perils of rocky soil as well as thorny soil. Seeds will sprout but not prosper there. The life of the plant gets choked and wounded by the rocks and thorns. These soils, according to Jesus, receive the seed but trouble is not far behind. Trouble shows up because soil crowded with rocks and thorns is not healthy soil. Attention must be given to these so that the life of the plant (the believer) can produce fruit. Jesus also described a fourth soil. The fourth soil is good and ready to host strong healthy plants that produce.

As those who have received the seed, the Word of God, you and I must pay close attention to the condition of our hearts. According to Christ, a heart that is fearful allows affliction and persecution to rob it of the joy that once characterized its faith. A heart that is anxious and covetous allows worries and wealth to block fruitfulness. A heart that is healthy receives the Word and then experiences great growth.

Let's be like the diligent farmer who carefully watches over the soil. If you find the soil of your heart is hard-packed and unreceptive, consider softening the soil by allowing God's Spirit to break through the hardness. If you have never received the truth then I encourage you to do so today. Do not allow the seed that is meant to sprout and produce fruit become bird food. If you find your heart crowded with fear, anxiety, covetousness, worries, or affection for wealth, allow God's Spirit to pull out those thorns and rocks that block the growth. There is great joy in bearing fruit thirty-, sixty-, and a hundredfold. Farmers call that a good year and Jesus calls it a good life. Let's call it both!

A Life That Shines

And He was saying to them, "A lamp is not brought to be put under a basket, is it, or under a bed? Is it not [brought] to be put on the lampstand? For nothing is hidden, except to be revealed; nor has [anything] been secret, but that it would come to light. If anyone has ears to hear, let him hear." And He was saying to them, "Take care what you listen to. By your standard of measure it will be measured to you; and more will be given you besides. "For whoever has, to him [more] shall be given; and whoever does not have, even what he has shall be taken away from him."

MARK 4:21–25

IN HIS EXPLANATION of the soils, Jesus clearly said that persecution and affliction would arise because of the Word. I believe He was beginning to cast a vision, for those willing to hear, of what life can be like in the midst of those difficulties. Now that they were given an understanding of the negatives associated with "rocky soil" (a fearful heart) and "thorny soil" (an anxious and covetous heart), they were given a vision for a life that would continue to grow strong and fruitful and thus *shine*.

Simply put, a life that *shines* reflects the character of God. A life that reflects the character of God will be rewarded. Just as you and I would never light a lamp and hide it under a bed, we must never allow our life in Christ to be hidden.

Jesus came to give us the fullness of life. The living Word implanted in our hearts has everything we need to experience that fullness but there is still a growing process involved. As our relationship with Him grows, our lives experience an increase in Christ-like qualities such as "love, joy, peace, patience, kindness, goodness, faithfulness, gentleness, self-control . . ." (the "fruit of the Spirit" as described in Galatians 5:22–23).

This kind of life must not be a secret. It must be revealed to the world so that the world may know there is hope. There are lots of voices with lots of messages out there. Jesus warns that we must be careful what we listen to. If we fail to listen to His voice of reason, we lose. If we choose to listen to His voice of reason, we win.

As we consider the meaning of this passage for us today, let's look at where we have placed our "lamp." If it is tucked away behind anything offensive to God (sin . . . there, I said it!) then the purpose of the lamp is defeated. If it is hidden under a pile of bitterness, resentment, unresolved anger, fear, anxiety, or any other emotional baggage, then the *shine* is definitely blocked. Just as He desires to see the plant produce fruit, Jesus desires to see the lamp *shine*. He told His friends one day, "Let your light shine before men in such a way that they may see your good works, and glorify your Father who is in heaven" (Matthew 5:16). That is not an impossible assignment, you know; it is what we have been designed to do. We were designed to live life in such a way that we *shine*. To *shine* in such a way that people think good things about our Father. In the end, that's all that really matters.

While We Were Asleep

And He was saying, "The kingdom of God is like a man who casts seed upon the soil; and he goes to bed at night and gets up by day, and the seed sprouts and grows—how, he himself does not know. The soil produces crops by itself; first the blade, then the head, then the mature grain in the head. But when the crop permits, he immediately puts in the sickle, because the harvest has come."

MARK 4:26–29

THE KINGDOM OF God was at hand and the followers of Christ needed a good understanding or explanation of that kingdom. To understand the kingdom itself would help those privileged to be kingdom dwellers.

We learn from Jesus that the kingdom of God has both a known and unknown aspect. The known aspect is about the "what" of the kingdom. The known has to do with the *sprouting* of life, the *growth* of life, the *fruit* of life, and the *harvest* of life. These are all things we can see. Jesus uses a word picture that his friends would immediately relate to since most of them grew up around farms. Through this word picture, they learn of a kingdom that is about life—from start to finish, the kingdom of God is about life.

The unknown aspect of the kingdom has to do with the "how" of the kingdom. The ground produces the crops and the crops grow but all of this happens as the farmer is sleeping. An invisible force is at work in the field. So the friends of Jesus learn the kingdom of God has both a physical (visible) as well as a spiritual (invisible) element.

Attention all kingdom dwellers! You and I belong to a spiritual kingdom that is about the start and growth of life by the power of God, not man. While we can see and enjoy the fruit of the growth, there is an element to the kingdom that we cannot see. We must get used to the fact that God is at work causing growth whether we see and feel Him or not.

This may be hard for our more "controlling" friends to hear but we all need to be reminded that growth does not happen by pulling on the stalk. This is true in our lives as well as the lives of our children. God the invisible One is at work in the field. God is at work in the lives of His children. God is at work in His kingdom. We are alive because of Him and we will grow because of Him. If we try to figure things out beyond that, we will inadvertently trample upon a deep and holy mystery. Instead of trying to pull on stalks as a means of experiencing growth, let's allow God to be God. Let's go to bed early a few nights this week and let Him be in charge.

When you think about it, going to bed and pulling the sheets over you is really just practice for the yet-to-be-revealed day the coffin lid closes over you. Sleeping is how we practice dying. It is how we practice dying to self. Going to sleep not only gives our bodies needed rest, it gets us out of God's way. Let's start going to bed a little earlier this week and when we wake up, go out into the field and marvel at the growth. And to think, it all happened while we were asleep . . . how about that!

The Underdog of Seeds

And He said, "How shall we picture the kingdom of God, or by what parable shall we present it? [It is] like a mustard seed, which, when sown upon the soil, though it is smaller than all the seeds that are upon the soil, yet when it is sown, it grows up and becomes larger than all the garden plants and forms large branches; so that THE BIRDS OF THE AIR can NEST UNDER ITS SHADE."

With many such parables He was speaking the word to them, so far as they were able to hear it; and He did not speak to them without a parable; but He was explaining everything privately to His own disciples.

MARK 4:30–34

WITH AN INTRICATE two-question introduction, Jesus tells us that the formation and growth of God's kingdom is similar to what happens to the mustard seed (the common black mustard seed). The black mustard seed is so small that it would take about 750 seeds to weigh a gram (28 grams equal an ounce). When you do the math, you realize it takes about 21,000 mustard seeds to muster one ounce. That is one small seed!

Don't make the mistake, however, of underestimating the mustard seed. It is the underdog of seeds; and we must never underestimate the underdog ... that's the one that surprises us. Once that tiny seed leaves the hand of the sower and falls to the ground, it dies. Still, don't count this little seed out just yet. Because it's when the seed dies that things really get good. You see, the mustard seed sprouts and grows into an enormous shrub reaching as high as 10–12 feet—all within just a few weeks.

The great thing about the mustard plant is that its strong expansive branches provide shade and shelter for the birds. Weary birds find rest in the branches of the mustard plant and threatened birds find needed protection as well. The heat of the day and the long journeys of flight take their toll on the birds of the air. They can't stay in the air the whole time so they look for safe places to land for shade and rest.

The kingdom of God is just such a place. Jesus, the underdog of rescuers by way of man's rejection and crucifixion of Him, lay dead in the ground for three days. Once dead, people saw Him as small and insignificant when it came to His claims of being the world's savior. But just as the tiny mustard seed came to life in the rich warm soil of Galilee, the Son of God came to life in the dark dampness of a Jerusalem cemetery. The kingdom's King is alive! Ezekiel 17:23 describes the promised Messiah as being like a strong cedar tree. "On the high mountain of Israel I will plant it, that it may bring forth boughs and bear fruit and become a stately cedar. And birds of every kind will nest under it; they will nest in the shade of its branches."

Take a quick assessment of your journey of faith. If you find you are a bit weary from the flight, allow yourself to land in the strong branches provided by Jesus. The King is in His kingdom providing protection for His people. Whether you see that as a castle, a cedar tree, or a mustard tree doesn't really matter. We know that the mustard tree begins with the underdog of seeds and grows to a whopping 10–12 feet! The kingdom of God started with the underdog of saviors and has grown to an enormous size. There is room for you and me to find rest and protection.

One of the reasons I like the story of the mustard seed is because it gives hope to an underdog like me. Weary from the flight and in desperate need of the safety of the sheltering branches of the King, this little bird finds his place. Keep in mind that there is plenty of room for you too!

The Monologue of a Storm

On that day, when evening came, He said to them, "Let us go over to the other side." Leaving the crowd, they took Him along with them in the boat, just as He was; and other boats were with Him. And there arose a fierce gale of wind, and the waves were breaking over the boat so much that the boat was already filling up. Jesus Himself was in the stern, asleep on the cushion; and they woke Him and said to Him, "Teacher, do You not care that we are perishing?" And He got up and rebuked the wind and said to the sea, "Hush, be still." And the wind died down and it became perfectly calm. And He said to them, "Why are you afraid? How is it that you have no faith?" They became very much afraid and said to one another, "Who then is this, that even the wind and the sea obey Him?"

MARK 4:35–41

❧

THE PROCESS OF knowing Jesus better continued with an invitation to cross the sea of Galilee. The simple phrase, "Let us go . . ." reminds us that God is calling us to venture with Him in the journey of faith and life. It speaks of the relationship He calls us to. The disciples were in the same boat as God and yet they did not fully realize who they were with. This can be the same for you and me in our journeys with Him.

A fierce storm overtook them and not only raised the waves to terrifying heights, but raised serious concerns and questions in the hearts and minds of the disciples. The concern was for "life and limb," and the question was whether or not Jesus cared about either. There was a sinking boat with panicked men doing all they could to bail water, and yet Jesus was asleep in the back of the boat. They were in a battle against nature and nature was winning. They were terrified by the way things were shaping up.

Victor Hugo described life as sometimes being as "terrifying as the monologue of a storm." So far, this storm was the only one speaking. It was a one-way communication because it had overpowered the men, and they had nothing to say that would appease the raging winds. They may have been screaming, but their screams held no power.

Who will speak for us? The Teacher has said a lot up to now; what does He say? Asleep? How could He be asleep at a time like this? Wake Him up!

It is the calmed soul that sleeps in the midst of the raging storm. It is the Creator of the elements who is able to rest while the elements are in turmoil. What does His nap communicate to us? What is the message? Beyond the obvious fact that He was really tired, the message is that our Creator is in control.

It is when Jesus awoke that the monologue ended. The Creator spoke three simple but powerful words into the raging storm, "Hush, be still."

Be encouraged by the fact that you are not on this journey of faith alone. The journey began when you responded to the invitation that started with, "Let us go . . ." No doubt the storms of life that *have* overtaken or *are* overtaking you are fierce. Surely you know the terror of the monologue. Your screams and your efforts at bailing are useless. So now let me encourage you to let the Creator speak *for* you. Allow Him to utter those three powerful words, "Hush, be still."

On that fateful day, the disciples became keenly aware that Jesus was much more than a teacher. They started to ask, "Who then is this, that even the wind and the sea obey Him?" Is it not awesome that you and I are privileged to know that He is God? Is it not also awesome that you and I are privileged to be in the same boat with Him? That thought is so calming to my soul that I am ready to let Him do all the talking during the next storm. I think that while He is doing that, I will lie down and rest.

A Cry For Mercy

They came to the other side of the sea, into the country of the Gerasenes. When He got out of the boat, immediately a man from the tombs with an unclean spirit met Him, and he had his dwelling among the tombs. And no one was able to bind him anymore, even with a chain; because he had often been bound with shackles and chains, and the chains had been torn apart by him and the shackles broken in pieces, and no one was strong enough to subdue him. Constantly, night and day, he was screaming among the tombs and in the mountains, and gashing himself with stones. Seeing Jesus from a distance, he ran up and bowed down before Him; and shouting with a loud voice, he said, "What business do we have with each other, Jesus, Son of the Most High God? I implore You by God, do not torment me!" For He had been saying to him, "Come out of the man, you unclean spirit!" And He was asking him, "What is your name?" And he said to Him, "My name is Legion; for we are many." And he [began] to implore Him earnestly not to send them out of the country. Now there was a large herd of swine feeding nearby on the mountain. [The demons] implored Him, saying, "Send us into the swine so that we may enter them." Jesus gave them permission. And coming out, the unclean spirits entered the swine; and the herd rushed down the steep bank into the sea, about two thousand [of them]; and they were drowned in the sea.

MARK 5:1–13

THE JOURNEY ACROSS the lake apparently was made for a single tortured soul. Jesus traveled across the lake and through the storm for just one man. We see that He stepped out of the boat and found a man who was choosing to live among the dead. Not just one demon was having its way with this man, there were many. Friends and family had given up on this young man because it was clear to them there was nothing or no one who could subdue him. It is interesting to note that he came to Jesus begging not to be tortured. He came to Jesus needing grace and mercy.

While we may not have a legion of demons driving us into the tombs, we oftentimes have a legion of issues, problems, fears, and frustrations that can drive us into a lonely and miserable retreat from life. Some people find that their issues, problems, fears, and frustrations are quite manageable. Many times they are able to think and reason their way through problems as they seek the advice of friends and family. They see these issues as "do-able" and so they are never forced to go to the Lord for needed grace and mercy.

Oftentimes, the legion of issues, problems, fears and frustrations is too much. "Chains and shackles" can't hold them back. They can overwhelm us to the point that we are searching for grace and screaming for mercy. Oftentimes the overwhelming quantity of life's issues and problems is what God uses to draw us to Himself. When people depend on God's grace and mercy rather than on their own abilities, great things happen. A great turn-around takes place at the very moment of surrender.

It seems that the Scriptures show us it is God's grace that relieves man's guilt while it is God's mercy that relieves man's misery. It was by the grace of God that this tortured soul even had a second chance at life (through grace). It was by the mercy of God that this tortured soul even had a chance to *enjoy* that life. I believe this tortured soul received both that day.

If you find yourself weighted down with the guilt brought on by a life lived apart from God, then come out of "the tombs" and receive God's grace. If you have known God's grace in your life and find you are in misery due to issues, problems, fears, and frustrations, then call out for mercy. Surrendering or *giving in* is not the same as *giving up*. Only in our cry for God's mercy do we actually have any chance at all of enjoying the new life given to us by His grace.

Are You Pushing Him Away?

Their herdsmen ran away and reported it in the city and in the country. And [the people] came to see what it was that had happened. They came to Jesus and observed the man who had been demon-possessed sitting down, clothed and in his right mind, the very man who had had the "legion"; and they became frightened. Those who had seen it described to them how it had happened to the demon-possessed man, and [all] about the swine. And they began to implore Him to leave their region. As He was getting into the boat, the man who had been demon-possessed was imploring Him that he might accompany Him. And He did not let him, but He said to him, "Go home to your people and report to them what great things the Lord has done for you, and [how] He had mercy on you." And he went away and began to proclaim in Decapolis what great things Jesus had done for him; and everyone was amazed.

MARK 5:14–20

❧

To SAVE THE life of one tortured soul in the grips of a legion of demons, a herd of two thousand pigs was sacrificed. The entire herd dove off the cliff as the legion of demons left the man and entered the pigs. (Some say the pigs did a "swine-dive" but I think they were built more for the "cannon ball" . . . sorry!) The herdsmen were furious at the waste. They were outraged that their source of revenue literally took a dive off a cliff. They went into town to report the "terrible" thing Jesus had done.

When the townspeople came back to see what all the fuss was about, they found the man in his right mind, clothed and sitting calmly. They found a man rescued from death and restored to life. While everyone there should have celebrated the great turn-around, instead they asked Jesus to leave . . . immediately! They began pushing Him away. What were they thinking? Why respond that way? Did they truly believe the pigs were more valuable to God than this precious soul? Were the pigs more valuable to *them* than this man? Did they not remember that this was some mother's son given back her? Did they not realize that a whole family could now enjoy the one who once chose to leave them and live among the dead? Why would they not invite Jesus to come into their homes and share with them and their families the truth and power behind this great turn-around? Why push Him away?

I think I know why. Verse fifteen tells us that it was because of fear. Fear is the great thief of life and joy. When people are afraid they are imprisoned. Prison is the thief of freedom as fear is the thief of life and joy. It seems they were afraid of being *near* Jesus when in fact they should have been afraid of being *separated* from Him.

I remember reading the account of the rescue of Jessica McClure from the abandoned well in Midland, Texas, on October 16, 1987. The man who went into the shaft to rescue her was surprised when she pushed him away. Her fear was actually getting in the way of her rescue and freedom.

In our passage today, the people's Rescuer had arrived and they were pushing Him away. This was true for all but one, however. Look at the passage closely and you will see that the man who had been freed from the legion of demons wanted to go with Jesus. Notice also that Jesus would not let him. Why? It was now time for the man to go home to be with his family. Jesus told him to go home to his people and report what great things the Lord had done for him. *Go tell them how I had mercy on you!*

Is fear robbing you of life and joy? If so, what is it that frightens you? What scares you about allowing Christ to come close? Is it the loss of something as valuable to you as the two thousand pigs were to those townsfolk? Are you afraid you will miss that "thing of value"? If so, let me encourage you to take your eyes and heart off that thing of value and focus on the Rescuer who is of infinite value. The Rescuer has arrived to set things right. Rejoice! Celebrate! Party! Make some noise! Anything but push Him away. He has had mercy on you . . . tell someone!

We Can't Save Our Children

When Jesus had crossed over again in the boat to the other side, a large crowd gathered around Him; and so He stayed by the seashore. One of the synagogue officials named Jairus came up, and on seeing Him, fell at His feet and implored Him earnestly, saying, "My little daughter is at the point of death; [please] come and lay Your hands on her, so that she will get well and live." And He went off with him; and a large crowd was following Him and pressing in on Him.

MARK 5:21–24

I AM NOT sure where many of us got the notion that we can save our children, but no doubt the notion is ours. Somewhere along the line many of us got *training, loving, directing, helping,* and *nurturing* confused with *saving*! I think that is why we are so devastated when we find out they are in trouble. *All our work for naught? Is that how it all plays out after years of parenting?*

Jairus had, most assuredly, done all he could do to save his little girl. He had done all he could to bring her back to health, but she was dying and he was helpless to save her. If you and I have not experienced the same situation on a physical level, there is absolutely no doubt in my mind we have faced it on a spiritual level. There are many of us who have been crushed by the reality that we cannot do more (or anything, for that matter) to save our child, spouse, friend, or others who are dear to us.

So what do we do? I believe we must add something to our training, loving, directing, helping, and nurturing. I believe we must do what Jairus did—entrust our children to their Creator. Think about it, the One who had the power to create is the One who has the power to rescue. You and I do not have the power to do either. Let's accept that and move on. Jairus sought out Jesus in a crowd and expressed his desperate need. Jairus, the great and powerful synagogue official, was forced to admit that he was powerless in this dire strait. *Please, my little girl is dying and I need You!* Why is that so hard for us to admit? Are we so sure of our skills and abilities to rescue that we cannot admit our need? Or is it that we are in the habit of rescuing our children? Whatever it is, let's stop!

There is a good chance there is someone in your life for whom you have exhausted yourself, and maybe even your resources, to save. I would like to see you give yourself permission to cease and desist. Admit that the great and powerful mom in you is all tuckered out. Admit that the great and powerful dad, husband, wife, grandma, or friend is empty.

It is only at that point that you and I will fall at the feet of the Creator and ask Him to do that which only He can do ... *Please come and lay Your hands on this one I desperately love, so that they will get well and live.* At that point, it is all up to Him.

Remember, there is a difference between things like *training, loving, directing, helping,* and *nurturing* (all things we are empowered to do) and *saving* (something we are not empowered to do)! Jairus realized this, and I am confident we can, too.

A Simple Touch of Faith

A woman who had had a hemorrhage for twelve years,
and had endured much at the hands of many physicians,
and had spent all that she had and was not helped at all,
but rather had grown worse—after hearing about Jesus,
she came up in the crowd behind [Him] and touched
His cloak. For she thought, "If I just touch His garments,
I will get well." Immediately the flow of her blood was
dried up; and she felt in her body that she was healed of
her affliction. Immediately Jesus, perceiving in Himself
that the power [proceeding] from Him had gone forth,
turned around in the crowd and said, "Who touched My
garments?" And His disciples said to Him, "You see the
crowd pressing in on You, and You say, 'Who touched
Me?'" And He looked around to see the woman who had
done this. But the woman fearing and trembling, aware
of what had happened to her, came and fell down before
Him and told Him the whole truth. And He said to her,
"Daughter, your faith has made you well; go in peace and
be healed of your affliction."

MARK 5:25–34

A CERTAIN WOMAN was bleeding to death and the doctors couldn't
help her. The cycle—which should have lasted a few days once a
month and then stopped—kicked in twelve years earlier and didn't
stop. She had been suffering ever since. The doctor bills kept being
delivered though the cure never was. What could she have been
thinking at that point? *What about this Jesus I keep hearing about? I
have heard He has power to heal. What if He can do what no one else
has been able to do?*

As she moved in closer to Jesus, she realized that the crowd was
enormous. He was not only hard to get to, but He was busy help-

ing so many other people. She may or may not have known He was actually on His way to the home of the great and powerful Jairus. *What makes me think Jesus would take the time to deal with my misery?* She may have decided that she did not need His full attention. She was obviously convinced that Jesus had the power to heal her. She was so convinced that Jesus was full of healing power, she simply needed to touch His clothes. And so she did.

That was when she got what may have been the surprise of her life—He noticed! Not only did He notice, but He stopped to find out more about the one He noticed. Once she came forward with the truth that she was the one, she received yet another shock—He listened! The busy God of all creation took the time to listen to her *whole* story. Jesus did not rush her through the needless details. He did not ask her to give the abbreviated version. He took the time to listen to her story. Everything she wanted to share, she shared. The crowd had to wait. That parade stopped for just one. This hurting woman had the full attention of God.

There are lots of things in life that will naturally surprise you and me. I hope we are not surprised to learn that our whole story is important to God. He has the time to hear you out. He also has the interest to hear you out. Most importantly, however, He has the power to make a difference. Even when no one else will take the time to listen to you and me, the Lord will. Even when you and I "endure much at the hands of many" and our condition has grown worse, the Lord's power is available to us.

Let's be surprised when the weather suddenly changes. Let's be surprised when we get a refund from the IRS. Let's be surprised when the boss pats us on the back and says, "Way to go!" But let's not be surprised when God notices us, takes the time to listen to us, and offers His power by way of a simple touch of faith.

The Journey Is Just Starting

While He was still speaking, they came from the [house of] the synagogue official, saying, "Your daughter has died; why trouble the Teacher anymore?" But Jesus, overhearing what was being spoken, said to the synagogue official, "Do not be afraid [any] [longer], only believe." And He allowed no one to accompany Him, except Peter and James and John the brother of James. They came to the house of the synagogue official; and He saw a commotion, and [people] loudly weeping and wailing. And entering in, He said to them, "Why make a commotion and weep? The child has not died, but is asleep." They [began] laughing at Him. But putting them all out, He took along the child's father and mother and His own companions, and entered [the room] where the child was. Taking the child by the hand, He said to her, "*Talitha kum!*" (which translated means, "Little girl, I say to you, get up!"). Immediately the girl got up and [began] to walk, for she was twelve years old. And immediately they were completely astounded. And He gave them strict orders that no one should know about this, and He said that [something] should be given her to eat.

MARK 5:35–43

WHAT IS IT going to take to get you and me used to the idea that death for a believer is a beginning much more than it is an ending? What will it take to convince us that death is when the most exciting part of the journey actually starts?

In the passage today, we are introduced to a crowd of people who were gripped by despair over a life cut short. A life cut very short at twelve years old. To them, her journey ended before it really even got started. From their limited perspective, Jesus could head home because it was too late. The train, so to speak, had pulled into the station and the engineer had gone home. The journey was over. *Everyone please watch your head and be sure you have gathered all of your belongings as you exit to your right. Also, if the last one out could turn off the lights, that would be great.*

Wait a minute, not so fast! That is how it looks from the human perspective when God is left out. But what about the way God sees it? What does death mean when He is involved? To see it His way takes one thing and one thing only—faith. "Do not be afraid any longer, only believe" (Mark 5:36). Jesus is offering us the eternal perspective on death. From His point of view, that little girl was asleep. Now, do we laugh or do we laud? Do we mock or do we marvel? Do we ridicule or do we rejoice?

The fact of the matter is this little girl's journey took on a new excitement and exhilaration right after she died. Her journey really began with the touch and words of Jesus as He took her hand in His and whispered in her ear, something to the effect of, *Get up little one. You have a big day ahead of you. Let's get you something to eat. You will need your strength for what lies ahead.*

I am not sure how much you have allowed yourself to think about your own death lately. Allow me to encourage you with this thought. With Christ holding your hand and whispering in your ear, it is the *start* of a wonderful adventure and journey. Death for a believer is not about the train pulling *into* the station. It is about the train pulling *out* of the station. "Do not be afraid any longer, only believe."

On that wonderful day, I wonder if we won't hear something along the lines of, *Please sit back and put on your seat belt. Be sure to look out the window because the journey you are about to embark on is going to show you some wonderful things. Enjoy!*

He Wondered At Their Unbelief

Jesus went out from there and came into His hometown;
and His disciples followed Him. When the Sabbath
came, He began to teach in the synagogue; and the many
listeners were astonished, saying, "Where did this man
[get] these things, and what is [this] wisdom given to
Him, and such miracles as these performed by His hands?
Is not this the carpenter, the son of Mary, and brother of
James and Joses and Judas and Simon? Are not His sisters
here with us?" And they took offense at Him. Jesus said
to them, "A prophet is not without honor except in his
hometown and among his [own] relatives and in his [own]
household." And He could do no miracle there except that
He laid His hands on a few sick people and healed them.
And He wondered at their unbelief.

And He was going around the villages teaching.

MARK 6:1–6

To BE WITHOUT honor in one's country is one thing, but to be without honor in your own hometown, among relatives, and in your
own household, must have even a deeper sting to it. Jesus had to
endure what some may consider the most painful of rejections
when he was faced with the rejection of his hometown, relatives,
and family.

In this passage, we find the Savior of the world imparting truth
(teaching) to a large crowd of listeners which contained a few believers. We find the Great Physician in town and evidence of only a
few people of faith. He healed few because few believed. "He wondered at their unbelief" (Mark 6:6).

What was keeping these folks from placing their faith in Him?
Was it His seemingly familiar origin? They knew His mother and
father. They knew His four brothers and His unnamed sisters.

They saw Him grow up from the time He was a baby. *So where did He get the wisdom? Where did He get the ability to perform such miracles?* Those hands they once watched build cabinets now raised the dead. The hands they once witnessed putting furniture together were now putting bodies back together. This common carpenter did some uncommon things . . . but *how* He did them was a mystery to them.

Let's not make the same mistake these townspeople made. Christ is not common and His origin is not natural. He is the God of the universe who is all-powerful. He is God and we are designed to live our lives with Him in faith.

Jesus, the Mighty One, did not try to win them over with feats of magic. He did not try to win their affection and loyalty by performing for them. He lived among them and called them to faith. Their lack of faith caused them to miss out on the power of God. He was with them. He taught them. He astonished them. But bottom line, He offended them. What was the offense? You can almost see it in the headlines of the local paper. *Local Boy Claims To Be God. Local Carpenter Makes Bold Claims Along With Cabinets.*

We must not simply be listeners who are astonished. We must be disciples who follow. The crowd recognized His wisdom and His power. The words and works of Christ did not go unnoticed. They did, however, go unaccepted. The words and works of Christ lay unappropriated by mere "listeners." Christ has been calling for those with ears to *hear*, not just to *listen*. Christ is calling for disciples who follow. Since faith sees the power of God, let's keep our hearts open in faith and our eyes open in wonder. Let's not make Him be the only one who wonders . . . at least not at our unbelief!

Walking Tools

And He summoned the twelve and began to send them
out in pairs, and gave them authority over the unclean
spirits; and He instructed them that they should take
nothing for [their] journey, except a mere staff—no bread,
no bag, no money in their belt—but [to] wear sandals; and
[He added], "Do not put on two tunics." And He said to
them, "Wherever you enter a house, stay there until you
leave town. Any place that does not receive you or listen to
you, as you go out from there, shake the dust off the soles
of your feet for a testimony against them." They went out
and preached that [men] should repent. And they were
casting out many demons and were anointing with oil
many sick people and healing them.

MARK 6:7–13

ASSIGNMENTS WERE GIVEN. Partners were assigned. Authority was
granted. It was time for the disciples to venture out into the surrounding region with the same message Jesus had given to them.
They were going in pairs to tell a lost and broken world that God
had come to rescue them. They were taking the most exciting story
ever told to a world that desperately needed to hear it. But it would
not be easy. As a matter of fact, Jesus gave them instructions that
ensured they would have to depend on God alone.

They could not take a bag. They could not take bread or money.
They were not allowed to take a change of clothes. They *could* wear
sandals and they *could* carry a stick. It is interesting that the physical tools they were given were for walking. The message was clear
. . . Go! If they had any idea that following and obeying Jesus was
going to be easy, they just found out they were wrong.

They were told to go into a town, find a welcoming home and
stay put. Jesus was allowing this one fortunate home to have the

great blessing of being used by Him to provide for the needs of His friends. The disciples had the great blessing of being served as they served others . . . kind of like a healthy community should be. Meeting needs of others is the definition of *agape* love. That was not a lesson to be learned in the classroom. It was a lesson to be learned in the field. And the field is where the disciples were headed.

The disciples were empowered to defeat spiritual beings that opposed them. How exciting that must have been to have that kind of power as they faced hostile forces. They were given direct orders by their Commander to go into the battlefield ready to depend on Him. They were to take nothing but that which would help them walk into the battlefield. They went and they shared the truth of God's redemptive plan. Obviously some would believe and some would not. *What do we do if they don't listen to us, Jesus? What if they reject the truth?* Jesus' answer and instruction to them contained a visual effect. They were to literally shake the dust off their feet before they left. This certain act was a way of saying, *We have done what we were told to do and we now leave you in your own filth. We came to offer a pure and clean start, but you have said no!* Theirs was to be a visual rebuke.

Here are a couple of thoughts for today. First, if there is anything of "filth" in your life, if your thoughts and words don't match the message of Christ, if your actions are less than stellar in the area of sexual purity, if your words to others are less than kind and clean, consider a pure and clean start. Second, remember that you have been sent into the world with a powerful message just as the disciples had been. What will it take to accomplish? It will take a desperate dependence on God. It is a journey that takes faith and walking tools. We may want to take lots of supplies, but Christ won't allow it. Walk in faith. Depend on Christ. *Accept* the message of a clean and pure start, and then *tell* the story of a clean and pure start.

Are We Haunted By Our Past?

And King Herod heard [of it], for His name had become
well known; and [people] were saying, "John the Baptist
has risen from the dead, and that is why these miraculous
powers are at work in Him." But others were saying, "He is
Elijah." And others were saying, "[He is] a prophet, like one
of the prophets [of old]." But when Herod heard [of it], he
kept saying, "John, whom I beheaded, has risen!"

MARK 6:14–16

❧

WORD ABOUT JESUS' powerful miracles had gotten to King Herod.
People were trying to explain the power behind the miracles to
themselves and to others; therefore, several options were given.
Options included His being John the Baptist, Elijah, or other for-
mer prophets raised from the dead. If it were John the Baptist, as
Herod believed, the king's past had come back to haunt him.

It is interesting how much power our past has over us. Herod,
whose conscience was surely bothering him, started hearing about
the power of Jesus. Because of that, another kind of power—the
power of his past sin—was beginning to drive his thought pro-
cesses. Jesus was doing things that could not be explained with "the
hand is quicker than the eye." Jesus had given life to a little girl just
after taking the life of a storm. Stories of His ability to teach, as
well as heal, were getting back to Herod, and an all out effort to
explain it brought Herod back to his own past. Herod was indeed a
powerful king, but his power showed up in his ability to kill a person, whereas Jesus' power was seen in His ability to bring a person
back to life. The contrast is remarkable.

Herod took the life of John the Baptist, and he probably didn't
sleep well after that. Though he did not swing the blade himself,
he might as well have. From his own mouth came the confession,
"John, whom *I* beheaded, has risen" (Mark 6:16; emphasis added).

It was not a dead prophet who had come to life, but rather it was the Creator, who was walking the earth restoring life. While one king was taking life, the real King was giving life. The one king could not sleep at night and the other was sleeping through storms. Again, the contrast is noticeable and striking.

What is in your past that needs to be confronted? As you consider the Giver of Life who stands ready to forgive, what comes to mind in the way of your wayward past? The sin in our lives has delivered many deathblows to relationships, opportunities to serve, chances to grow, and occasions to encourage. Is there anything keeping you up at night? Your guilt and mine are erased by receiving God's grace through faith. This is true whether our past goes back twenty-four years, months, days, hours, or seconds.

Instead of allowing our past to rise from the dead to torment us, let's embrace the risen Lord and allow Him to forgive us. He brings life, not death. He brings forgiveness, not guilt. Consider what Jean-Pierre de Caussade has said in *The Joy of the Saints*, "To escape the distress caused by regret for the past or fear about the future, this is the rule to follow: leave the past to the infinite mercy of God, the future to His good providence; give the present wholly to His love by being faithful to His grace." If that does not make for a good night's sleep, I am not sure what will.

The Rotten Fruit Of A Grudge

For Herod himself had sent and had John arrested and
bound in prison on account of Herodias, the wife of his
brother Philip, because he had married her. For John had
been saying to Herod, "It is not lawful for you to have
your brother's wife." Herodias had a grudge against him
and wanted to put him to death and could not [do so]; for
Herod was afraid of John, knowing that he was a righteous
and holy man, and he kept him safe. And when he heard
him, he was very perplexed; but he used to enjoy listening
to him. A strategic day came when Herod on his birthday
gave a banquet for his lords and military commanders
and the leading men of Galilee; and when the daughter of
Herodias herself came in and danced, she pleased Herod
and his dinner guests; and the king said to the girl, "Ask
me for whatever you want and I will give it to you." And
he swore to her, "Whatever you ask of me, I will give it to
you; up to half of my kingdom." And she went out and
said to her mother, "What shall I ask for?" And she said,
"The head of John the Baptist." Immediately she came in
a hurry to the king and asked, saying, "I want you to give
me at once the head of John the Baptist on a platter." And
although the king was very sorry, [yet] because of his oaths
and because of his dinner guests, he was unwilling to
refuse her. Immediately the king sent an executioner and
commanded [him] to bring [back] his head. And he went
and had him beheaded in the prison, and brought his head
on a platter, and gave it to the girl; and the girl gave it to
her mother. When his disciples heard [about this], they
came and took away his body and laid it in a tomb.

MARK 6:17–29

Herod Antipas was the king whose past had come back to haunt him. He was the one who had John the Baptist killed. His actions were the rotten fruit of a grudge.

Herod was married to the daughter of Aretas, the Arabian king of Petraea. Herod was intrigued with Herodias who was married to Philip I, Herod's half-brother, and decided to elope with her. They were both married to other people, and yet they married each other. This is why John the Baptist called them out. Herodias was angry about being confronted with this and developed a grudge. From that point on, she looked for an opportunity to get back at John.

The opportunity came at a birthday party Herod threw for himself. Herodias' daughter came to the party and ended up dancing for the crowd. The crowd was pleased, but not as much as Herod himself. Herod promised as a gift to the girl up to half his kingdom (the wine was definitely talking at this point). The response to this generous offer surely shocked and saddened the king. *I want the head of John the Baptist on a platter.* Herod was afraid of John because John's life was marked by holiness and righteousness. To take the life of this wonderful man, whom Herod enjoyed listening to and had been protecting, was nearly too much. But his word was given in front of his "lords and military commanders," and he could not back down.

The rotten fruit of a grudge was murder. The man who once enjoyed and protected John gave the order to execute him merely because the truth had been delivered, and the hearer (Herodias) was offended. A grudge developed and the plot to kill was the rotten fruit that followed.

Let's do a gut check right now. Is there a grudge we are holding on to? Is there a seed of bitterness toward someone who has spoken a difficult but true word to us? According to Jesus, to be angry about something like that is just like murder. We do not have to pull a trigger to be guilty of murder. We don't have to swing an ax blade at a person's neck to be counted guilty in this. All we have to do is say a hurtful word, make an inappropriate comment, select an opportune time to fire off an insult, and we are guilty of sin.

Christ has told us to reconcile with our brothers and sisters, and *then* bring offerings of sacrifice to the altar. A seed of bitterness leads to the root of anger, which leads to the stalk of hatred, which leads to the rotten fruit of a grudge, which is murder. Let's allow the Spirit of God to open our eyes to all such seeds of bitterness. Let's not let another day pass without dealing with this issue of grudges. Nothing good comes from that tree. Never has and never will!

A Planned Rest

The apostles gathered together with Jesus; and they reported to Him all that they had done and taught. And He said to them, "Come away by yourselves to a secluded place and rest a while." (For there were many [people] coming and going, and they did not even have time to eat.) They went away in the boat to a secluded place by themselves.

MARK 6:30–32

JESUS' FRIENDS HAD seen God do great things through their words and works, and they had exciting stories to tell. They came back to report to Jesus "all that they had done and taught" with the power and authority they had been given.

It is interesting to note that even with the power and authority of God in their lives, they still got tired. Because of this, Jesus had a planned rest for them. His plan was for them to move on to a quiet (i.e., remote or secluded) place to rest. The disciples were mere humans, and they needed to face the fact that the flesh and bone they had been given to serve the Lord was susceptible to getting worn down and worn out. They needed a planned rest, and Jesus was leading them toward one.

Jesus could tell they were weary and were in need of rest. Because of this weariness, Jesus gave the very important directive, "Come away by yourselves to a secluded place and rest" (Mark 6:31). His first directive had been to take their walking tools, along with a desperate dependence on God, and take the good news of God's redemptive power to the hurting world around them. His second directive was to walk away from the hectic needs of the world long enough to get some rest.

How are you doing with both of those directives? Are you doing well with one and not the other? Some of us are great at the work of God, and yet struggle when it comes to His call to rest. If that is true for you right now, let me encourage you to take Jesus seriously on both mandates. You and I will be of no long-term good to the Kingdom of God if we do not take time to rest. There will always be needs to meet. There will always be spiritual and physical hunger which requires us to provide food. If we do not obey Christ's call to rest, we will not finish the race and the battle into which He has called us.

The spiritual work of leading a family, a Bible study, a Sunday School class, a fellowship group, or just the life we've been given by Christ is wearisome. Sharing our faith at work and in the neighborhood takes spiritual energy. Our service to the Lord in the advancement of the Kingdom is going to wear us down. Jesus called His friends away to a secluded place to rest because they needed it. You and I are no different. We are human just as they were human. We need to rest just as they did.

Let me suggest a discipline you might want to consider for yourself. It is a discipline that includes the needed rest built into your life on a daily, weekly, monthly, and yearly basis. Develop the discipline of being alone with Jesus for a short period of time every day. Be alone in a secluded place with Jesus as you hear from Him in Scripture and speak to Him in prayer. Find a day each week (the Bible calls it a Sabbath rest) to stop working. Schedule a weekend a month to get away from the ordinary routine of work and home to focus on spiritual and physical rest. On a yearly basis, take all the vacation you are given at work. There is no need to leave those days on the table. They are a provision for you and your family to find rest and restoration together. The main thing is to have a planned rest. Jesus provided a planned rest for His friends and wants to provide it for you and me.

Who Will Lead and Feed You?

[The people] saw them going, and many recognized
[them] and ran there together on foot from all the cities,
and got there ahead of them. When Jesus went ashore,
He saw a large crowd, and He felt compassion for them
because they were like sheep without a shepherd; and He
began to teach them many things. When it was already
quite late, His disciples came to Him and said, "This place
is desolate and it is already quite late; send them away so
that they may go into the surrounding countryside and
villages and buy themselves something to eat." But He
answered them, "You give them [something] to eat!" And
they said to Him, "Shall we go and spend two hundred
denarii on bread and give them [something] to eat?" And
He said to them, "How many loaves do you have? Go
look!" And when they found out, they said, "Five, and two
fish." And He commanded them all to sit down by groups
on the green grass. They sat down in groups of hundreds
and of fifties. And He took the five loaves and the two fish,
and looking up toward heaven, He blessed [the food] and
broke the loaves and He kept giving [them] to the disciples
to set before them; and He divided up the two fish among
them all. They all ate and were satisfied, and they picked
up twelve full baskets of the broken pieces, and also of the
fish. There were five thousand men who ate the loaves.

MARK 6:33–44

❧

THOUGH THE PLAN was for the disciples to retreat to a secluded
spot for some much needed rest with Jesus, it did not happen—at
least not then. The crowd ran ahead and waited eagerly for more
direction and comfort from Jesus. The need was intense and so the
pursuit was intense. At this point, there was no rest for the weary.

70

Jesus' response to the crowd was one of divine compassion. The Greek word for *compassion* (*splagchnizomai*) is a word that literally means "to be moved in the inward parts." This means Jesus' stomach started to hurt when He saw this crowd he called "sheep without a shepherd." Jesus noticed the tragic fact that the people had to lead themselves, and He was moved.

The disciples had a different response. Instead of noticing the sheep's desperate need for a shepherd, they noticed the sun going down and their own stomachs hurting from hunger rather than compassion. They mentioned the people's need to head back into town for food, but I believe it was their own hunger they wanted satisfied. It seems to me that it was too easy for them to suggest that Jesus send the people away. Not only did the disciples want the people to *lead* themselves, they wanted them to *feed* themselves.

Jesus was not about to let that happen. "*You* give them something to eat" (Mark 6:37, emphasis added). In what tends to be a typical human reaction, the disciples started thinking in terms of money. *We cannot afford to feed all these people. Two hundred denarii won't even scratch the surface of what we need.* Two hundred denarii was the equivalent of eight months of a worker's salary. The median income for a family of four currently is just over $62,000. This means the disciples were estimating the need to be around $41,000 in today's U.S. dollars. *Not even $41,000 could feed all these people. Lord, send them home!*

Jesus continued to provide for both the disciples and the people. For the disciples who were apparently good at doing math in their heads, He provided a lesson in multiplication:

(Five loaves of bread) + (two fish) x (the power of God)
= compassion in action

For the people who were lost along the water's edge, Jesus provided a filling meal of bread and fish as they sat in small communities of hundreds and fifties. With a little bit of organization and a whole lot of passing the food around, over five thousand men were fed that afternoon. The way Mark recorded the account, only the men were counted. There is no way of telling, this side of glory, how many people in all were fed that day.

Please keep in mind that God never intended you and me to *lead* ourselves or *feed* ourselves. He is not only the shepherd, but He is the chef. He leads us and He feeds us because His compassion compels Him to provide. He doesn't provide just enough, either. The disciples felt the full brunt of His power to provide as they gathered twelve baskets of leftovers ... heavy baskets that scream testimony to the power of God to lead and feed. To whom will you look today for direction and nutrition? Is there a chance you could find yourself in a small community of people feeding on that which comes from the hand of the Shepherd? I sure hope so. It is getting late, you know ... so the disciples would say.

Take Courage

Immediately Jesus made His disciples get into the boat and go ahead of [Him] to the other side to Bethsaida, while He Himself was sending the crowd away. After bidding them farewell, He left for the mountain to pray.

When it was evening, the boat was in the middle of the sea, and He was alone on the land. Seeing them straining at the oars, for the wind was against them, at about the fourth watch of the night He came to them, walking on the sea; and He intended to pass by them. But when they saw Him walking on the sea, they supposed that it was a ghost, and cried out; for they all saw Him and were terrified. But immediately He spoke with them and said to them, "Take courage; it is I, do not be afraid." Then He got into the boat with them, and the wind stopped; and they were utterly astonished, for they had not gained any insight from the [incident of] the loaves, but their heart was hardened.

MARK 6:45–52

ONE OF THE great lessons of the "feeding of the five thousand" is that the compassion of God is not to be communicated as a concept. The compassion of God is to be communicated and demonstrated in the distribution of the provisions of God. As we see Jesus send His friends ahead in the boat, we see another lesson in His power as Creator take place. This time, instead of learning the lesson on land, they would learn the lesson on water. The God of land and sea was with them, and He was revealing Himself more and more.

I can't think of a better picture of what life is sometimes like for me. Straining at the oars while rowing a boat against the wind in rough water at night, while wondering where Jesus is, just about sums it up. I sometimes struggle with the feeling of being abandoned by God while wondering if I am even going the right direction. If that is how you sometimes feel, then I would like to encourage you with the truth that, though that is how it *feels*, that is not how it *is*!

Here is why I say that. Verse forty-eight has a phrase that has caught my attention and interest. It says, "... and He intended to pass by them." When I first read that, I thought He was trying to *bypass* them. But that is not what it says. It says He wanted to pass by them, like an Old Testament theophany, in order to reassure them. A theophany in the Old Testament was the appearance of God to people in a visible form. You can read about some of these theophanies in Exodus 33:19–22 and 1 Kings 19:11.

What a great time to be reassured—when they most needed it. But they did not recognize Him at first. As a matter of fact, their first response was terror as they cried out. They all thought they were seeing a ghost. It is in the midst of their terror that Jesus spoke the comforting words, "Take courage; it is I, do not be afraid." Jesus not only assured them with His words, He assured them with His presence. He climbed in the boat with them as if to say with His actions, *You are not alone on the water. You never were, and you never will be.* Don't forget that He saw them straining at the oars. They were never alone, even when they felt they were.

My prayer for you as you "struggle at the oars" in life today and this week is that you will take courage. Know that He is not only watching over you and wanting to reassure you, He is ready to identify Himself with the calming words, *It is I!* As a believer, you have the God of the Universe inside you. Not just in your "boat" but inside your very life.

The Divine presence in their boat brought a stop to the fear and a stop to the wind. The God of land and sea met them on the sea in a dark place as they struggled to make headway. Allow that same Divine presence to do the same thing in your life today. Amidst the darkness and the wind of life, I pray you hear Him say, "Take courage; it is I, do not be afraid."

The Hard Work of Prayer

When they had crossed over they came to land at
Gennesaret, and moored to the shore. When they got out
of the boat, immediately [the people] recognized Him, and
ran about that whole country and began to carry here and
there on their pallets those who were sick, to the place they
heard He was. Wherever He entered villages, or cities, or
countryside, they were laying the sick in the market places,
and imploring Him that they might just touch the fringe
of His cloak; and as many as touched it were being cured.

MARK 6:53–56

THE VILLAGES, CITIES and countryside were, as they are today, full
of people in need. Those who are emotionally, physically and spiritually ill are in tremendous pain and in need of the healing power of
Jesus Christ. But who will bring them to Jesus? Who will put them
in touch with the Savior?

The throngs recognized Jesus and ran home to get their friends
and families. They knew Jesus could heal their loved ones so they
scattered to retrieve those in desperate need.

Those who could not walk the long distances from the villages, cities and surrounding countryside were carried on pallets.
The strong arms and backs of friends lifted and carried the sick
and wounded long and difficult distances just so they would have
a chance to be made whole. It did not take much faith to see the
healing take place. Just to touch the fringe of His cloak was enough.
Faith wasn't the hard part of the journey. Carrying friends to Jesus
was the hard part.

If you and I acknowledge that Jesus is able to heal those who are
emotionally, physically and spiritually ill, then we have conquered
the easy part. It is easy to believe this about Jesus because we recognize Him for who He is, the Savior; and yet the hard part still

remains. The hard part oftentimes is the carrying of our friends and families to Jesus. We do not have to physically carry them to Jesus these days, although that might almost be easier than what we are called to do. We are called to carry them to the Lord in prayer. Why is that so hard? Why do we fail to consistently carry these precious people to the powerful Savior?

One reason may be that we are easily distracted by our *busyness*. We are busy people who are task-oriented and love to see the results of the work of our hands. Prayer is more difficult because we don't see results quickly. Without quick results our resolve to pray weakens. It is hard to keep at it when it comes to prayer because we get distracted.

Another reason may be that we are easily *discouraged*. Our friends and families won't admit their need so we become discouraged in prayer. Can you imagine what it would have been like if the young paralytic had verbally abused his four friends as they carried him to Jesus? Can you imagine him ridiculing them as they approached the Savior in faith? Imagine how discouraging it would have been for them to be cursed by their friend as they attempted to do something good. Discouragement keeps us from doing the hard work of prayer.

Another reason prayer is so difficult is that our lifestyles often *discredit* us in the eyes of non-believers and render our prayer life ineffective. It is one thing to announce our faith in Jesus to the world, but to live a life of faith in full view of the world is a totally different matter. If we are going to verbally testify to the merits of faith in Jesus, we must live a life that speaks louder than our words. "The effective prayer of a righteous man can accomplish much" (James 5:16).

Prayer is hard work. Carrying our friends and families to Jesus in prayer will take focus, courage and consistency of lifestyle. Now let's do the hard thing and start carrying folks to the Lord in prayer. Convinced of who He is, let's put people in front of the Savior. Let's break a sweat.

Put The Soap Down

The Pharisees and some of the scribes gathered around Him when they had come from Jerusalem, and had seen that some of His disciples were eating their bread with impure hands, that is, unwashed. (For the Pharisees and all the Jews do not eat unless they carefully wash their hands, [thus] observing the traditions of the elders; and [when they come] from the market place, they do not eat unless they cleanse themselves; and there are many other things which they have received in order to observe, such as the washing of cups and pitchers and copper pots.) The Pharisees and the scribes asked Him, "Why do Your disciples not walk according to the tradition of the elders, but eat their bread with impure hands?" And He said to them, "Rightly did Isaiah prophesy of you hypocrites, as it is written: 'THIS PEOPLE HONORS ME WITH THEIR LIPS, BUT THEIR HEART IS FAR AWAY FROM ME. BUT IN VAIN DO THEY WORSHIP ME, TEACHING AS DOCTRINES THE PRECEPTS OF MEN.' Neglecting the commandment of God, you hold to the tradition of men."

MARK 7:1–8

THE RELIGIOUS THUGS of the day, the Pharisees and some of the scribes (teachers of the Law), noticed that Jesus' disciples did not go through the traditional ceremonial cleansing before they ate lunch. The Jewish leadership of the day began trusting in the power of a bar of soap rather than in the power of God for the needed cleansing in their lives.

These religious leaders revealed a tremendous tragedy of their lives when they brought the matter of cleansing to Jesus' attention. Their religious duty and tradition became a means of making themselves acceptable to God. They were very proud of the fact that they would wash their hands after going to the market because they most likely came in contact with unclean food, utensils, and people. Thoroughly washing themselves several times a day was what they were trusting in to be acceptable to God.

I can only imagine the pain this caused Jesus . . . not because His friends were being attacked, but because He knew washing hands along with pots and pans had nothing to do with a right relationship with Him and His Father. I imagine His heart broke for all the millions of people in the world who believed, and continue to believe, they must clean themselves for God. His heart must have broken as He was able to name every single person in the world who was trapped in such despair; His heart breaking for all those who would continue to be trapped by the lie that they can make themselves acceptable to God with a bar of soap.

The enemy of God, Satan, has spread a dark and devastating lie throughout the world, and the world has been eager to believe it. The lie is that men and women can appease God by their works—works such as prayer a certain number of times a day, church attendance, giving money to the poor, not kicking the dog, or just being good (whatever that means). The problem with this is that no one is able to say when enough is enough. Because no one can say they have done enough, they must keep buying more soap. They live in fear of not ever being truly clean.

Jesus makes it very clear that to "behave" on the outside by saying the right things ("This people honors Me with their lips") while the inside is broken and distant ("but their heart is far away from Me . . .") is the real tragedy of life. The heart of man must be changed and the only way that can happen is through the grace of God. No human effort at washing the various parts of the body can change or clean a person's heart.

Consider this promise from God, "And I will *give* them one heart, and put a new spirit within them. And I will *take* the heart of stone out of their flesh and *give* them a heart of flesh, that they may walk in *My* statutes and keep *My* ordinances and do them" (Ezekiel 11:19–20, emphasis added). It is by the grace of God that we are able to receive the gift of a new heart and spirit that are able to keep *His* ordinances. In the area of being acceptable to God, the traditions of man are not to be trusted. Only God is able to make us acceptable to Himself. It is about God's grace, not man's works. What tradition, if any, are you trusting in to be acceptable to God? Trust only in Jesus Christ. It is then that your heart will be changed. It is only then that a true cleansing takes place. So put the soap down and trust only the Savior who is able to clean and change that which matters . . . your heart!

Truth Over Tradition

He was also saying to them, "You are experts at setting aside the commandment of God in order to keep your tradition. For Moses said, 'HONOR YOUR FATHER AND YOUR MOTHER'; and, 'HE WHO SPEAKS EVIL OF FATHER OR MOTHER, IS TO BE PUT TO DEATH'; but you say, 'If a man says to [his] father or [his] mother, whatever I have that would help you is Corban (that is to say, given [to God]),' you no longer permit him to do anything for [his] father or [his] mother; [thus] invalidating the word of God by your tradition which you have handed down; and you do many things such as that."

MARK 7:9–13

❧

IT IS NOT only dangerous but also tragic to set the Word of God aside and replace its authority with another. Though its significance is much greater in our lives than an "owner's manual," what we often do with the truth and authority of Scripture is similar to what many do with owner's manuals and instructions. Whether we are in too much of a hurry or we don't like being told what to do, we too easily discard the instructions.

Jesus confronted a group of people who wanted to live life their own way and refused to put themselves under the authority of the Scripture. Jesus could tell they had become experts in setting aside the commandments of God in order to keep their own traditions. The commandments of God, the whole of Scripture ". . . is inspired by God and profitable for teaching, for reproof, for correction, for training in righteousness; so that the man of God may be adequate, equipped for every good work" (2 Timothy 3:16–17).

The Bible is given to us to *teach* us God's truth. While we go to great lengths to find truth, we are told clearly in God's Word that He Himself is the source of truth. All that we believe must be measured against what comes from the lips of God. Truth of God must win out over the tradition of man. We also learn that the Scripture shows us—rebukes us—when we blow it. It calls the sin in our life exactly what it is: sin! It won't rename it so we can feel good about ourselves. The Word of God shows us where we have missed the mark and calls us to account. No wonder it is often set aside. It is too difficult for some to admit they have offended God with their choices and actions. One of the great things about God's Word is that it does not just show us where we are wrong but it *corrects* us, so we may go in the right direction. Our parents corrected us when we played in the street so that we could learn the safe places to play. Scripture does the same—it takes young believers and *trains* them in life. We are not left here to fend for ourselves. Scripture trains us to live a life that is full and abundant. That's why Jesus came in the flesh (John 10:10).

The "owner's manual" is not to be set aside; it's needed more today than ever before. You and I must not let the traditions of man replace the authority of God, or we will be even more confused about life than before. Traditions change, preferences come and go, desires to have it our own way will continue to cause fights, battles, and all-out war. Man's traditions have failed us in the past and will continue to fail us, but God's Word has never failed us. We can choose to put ourselves *over* His Word in judgment, picking and choosing what we will and will not accept; we can put ourselves *beside* it, making ourselves equal to its authority; or we can put ourselves *under* it, allowing the authority of God's Word to teach, reproof, correct and train us in life.

There was a man who scoffed that he had gone through the Bible five times and never saw a difference in his life. His friend replied, "Allow the Bible to go through *you* once and you will never be the same." Setting aside God's Word to live by man's traditions is not only dangerous, it is wrong. Jesus pointed this out over two thousand years ago, and it is still true today.

The Heart of the Matter

After He called the crowd to Him again, He [began] saying to them, "Listen to Me, all of you, and understand: there is nothing outside the man which can defile him if it goes into him; but the things which proceed out of the man are what defile the man. [If anyone has ears to hear, let him hear.]"

When he had left the crowd [and] entered the house, His disciples questioned Him about the parable. And He said to them, "Are you so lacking in understanding also? Do you not understand that whatever goes into the man from outside cannot defile him, because it does not go into his heart, but into his stomach, and is eliminated?" ([Thus He] declared all foods clean.) And He was saying, "That which proceeds out of the man, that is what defiles the man. For from within, out of the heart of men, proceed the evil thoughts, fornications, thefts, murders, adulteries, deeds of coveting [and] wickedness, [as well] [as] deceit, sensuality, envy, slander, pride [and] foolishness. All these evil things proceed from within and defile the man."

MARK 7:14–23

JESUS HAS MADE it clear to us that the problem between us and God is not an outward or physical issue. The problem between us and God is not about us failing to wash our hands before a meal (Mark 7:1–4) or failing to keep a certain tradition. Ceremonies and sacrifices don't matter to God because those external things don't address the real problem. The heart of the matter is just that ... the heart. Jesus desired the crowd to know that the heart of man is broken by rebellion against God.

He called the crowd to Himself to lay out the heart of the matter. He was calling people (all of them) to listen carefully and to understand. Nothing on the *outside* of man can defile the *inside* of man . . . because our insides are already defiled. Defiled means ruined or damaged. Our rebellion against God (demanding life be lived our way) ruins the relationship we were designed to live with God.

Sin in a person's heart is like a worm in an apple. How does a worm get inside an apple? Perhaps you think the worm burrows in from the outside. Actually, scientists have discovered that the worm comes from the *inside*. But how does he get in there? Simple! An insect lays an egg in the apple blossom. Sometime later, the worm hatches in the heart of the apple, then eats his way out. Sin, like the worm, begins in the heart and works its way out through a person's thoughts, words, and actions. This is what Jesus presented to those who insisted they could make themselves acceptable to God by their actions.

There are many people among us today who are weary of working their way back to God through ritual and ceremony. It seems that "the crowd" needs to hear the words of Christ on this matter. The insect has laid the egg on the blossom of our hearts and the worm has come out—looking like hate, obscenities, fear, lust, worry, greed, deceptions, arrogance, foolishness, and so much more. The only cure for this is the grace of God received in faith apart from works.

While religious people continue to waste time arguing over rituals, diets, ceremonies, and other human initiatives as the solution to their polluted lives, you and I have a chance to sit quietly before the Lord and hear the Good News of grace. The inward work of God touches the inward problem of the heart. The egg has hatched and the worm is loose. Ceremonies and rituals are powerless to kill the worm. Only the death and resurrection of Christ has the power to make a difference. This power is appropriated only by faith.

For those who are weary of working their way back to God through ritual and ceremony, know that you can stop and rest. Rest in the power and grace of God. It is the grace of God alone that will kill the worm. *If anyone has ears to hear, let him hear.*

The Children and the Dogs Have All Been Fed

Jesus got up and went away from there to the region of Tyre. And when He had entered a house, He wanted no one to know [of it]; yet He could not escape notice. But after hearing of Him, a woman whose little daughter had an unclean spirit immediately came and fell at His feet. Now the woman was a Gentile, of the Syrophoenician race. And she kept asking Him to cast the demon out of her daughter. And He was saying to her, "Let the children be satisfied first, for it is not good to take the children's bread and throw it to the dogs." But she answered and said to Him, "Yes, Lord, [but] even the dogs under the table feed on the children's crumbs." And He said to her, "Because of this answer go; the demon has gone out of your daughter." And going back to her home, she found the child lying on the bed, the demon having left.

MARK 7:24–30

❦

In leaving the borders of Galilee and going into the region of Tyre and Sidon (modern day Lebanon), Jesus and His disciples found a welcoming house and settled in for some much needed rest and private instruction. All other attempts to rest were foiled by the swarming crowds. This time, they left the country and found shelter in a private home. He didn't want their whereabouts known so they could get some uninterrupted time together.

While He was teaching His disciples (His children), a Gentile woman who had heard the news of His great compassion and capabilities interrupted. He could not escape notice, we are told. She humbled herself before Jesus and told of the misery her daughter was in because of the work or an unclean spirit. Mark makes a point of reminding us that she was a Gentile, of the Syrophoenician race. She was not a Jew and she was not a disciple. She was, however, a precious creation of God who was in need.

She came asking for help for her daughter. Jesus' response was appropriate to His reason for being there, and was spoken in a way the woman would understand. In other words, He did not speak over her head. His answer was given in figurative speech, and though it may sound insulting to us to refer to someone as a "dog," it was just the opposite. Jesus said, "Let the children be satisfied first, for it is not good to take the children's bread and throw it to the dogs" (Mark 7:27). The Greek word used here refers to "little dogs" which were house pets. He was not referring to wild, dirty dogs that dig around in trash cans. Jesus was letting her know that His first priority was to instruct His disciples whom He referred to as "children." It seems that Jesus was protecting that time and was asking this dear lady to wait.

The woman said something that I believe touched the heart of Jesus. She took His own analogy one step further. She pointed out that even house pets are able to eat at the *same time* the children do, since they eat the crumbs dropped by the children. Touché! I believe her reply touched the heart of Christ because she demonstrated humility (she replied "Yes, Lord") and faith. Again, it is faith that counts with God.

I hope you find it encouraging that Jesus desired to protect His time with His "children" and yet allowed the "outsider" to interrupt. I hope you find it encouraging that Jesus responded to this woman's humility and faith by providing relief for her daughter. Please consider your own relationship with Jesus today. Please know that there is room *at* the table and *under* the table of God for all of us. Jesus has provided so much for all of us, we can confidently say *The children and dogs have all been fed!*

So enjoy some quiet and private instruction from the Lord as you pray and read Scripture. Eat the full and delicious meal He sets before you. Let's not worry if some crumbs fall to the ground; we all have some friends (hungry puppies) who could feed on what we drop.

Are You Utterly Astonished?

Again He went out from the region of Tyre, and came
through Sidon to the Sea of Galilee, within the region
of Decapolis. They brought to Him one who was deaf
and spoke with difficulty, and they implored Him to lay
His hand on him. Jesus took him aside from the crowd,
by himself, and put His fingers into his ears, and after
spitting, He touched his tongue [with the saliva]; and
looking up to heaven with a deep sigh, He said to him,
"*Ephphatha!*" that is, "Be opened!" And his ears were
opened, and the impediment of his tongue was removed,
and he [began] speaking plainly. And He gave them orders
not to tell anyone; but the more He ordered them, the
more widely they continued to proclaim it. They were
utterly astonished, saying, "He has done all things well; He
makes even the deaf to hear and the mute to speak."

MARK 7:31–37

JESUS RETURNED TO the region of Decapolis (a grouping of ten
Greek cities of which all but one was East of the Jordan river). It is
the region in which Jesus had earlier healed the demoniac. It was in
this region that a group of people pleaded with him to touch a man
who was deaf and who could not speak very well. It is not unusual
for a lack of hearing to affect a person's speech. It is no surprise this
man struggled in both areas of his life.

I believe it was a true gesture of compassion for Jesus to take
this man aside from the crowd. This man needed some one-on-one
time with Jesus. This man also needed the personal and powerful
touch of the Messiah. This man received both that day. The crowd,
however, soon knew the results of Jesus' healing touch. The man
was able to clearly hear and plainly speak. With one Aramaic word
"Ephphatha," the ears of the man became completely open. With

one simple yet power-packed word, the tongue of the man became completely loosed. Mark tells us that the reaction from the crowd was one of utter astonishment.

I don't know about you, but when I first read this passage I was not "utterly astonished." It seemed natural, if not ordinary, to me that Jesus could and would do something like that. I wrestled with my response for a while and concluded that many of the stories I read (and reread) about Jesus are so familiar that my *astonishment* has definitely waned. It scares me that I have grown so used to the stories about Jesus that I am not easily astonished.

What is there *not* to be astonished about? The Creator has taken on flesh in the person of Jesus Christ and walked into a region of ten well-populated cities. From out of that enormous sea of people on the shores of the Sea of Galilee, He takes the hand of one very damaged man and leads him to an isolated spot. Once alone, Jesus (God incarnate) puts His fingers in the man's dead ears and touches the man's paralyzed tongue with His own spit and lets out a tremendous sigh. Divine compassion expressed through intimate contact and an audible sigh precedes the bringing to life of a set of ears and the letting loose of a tongue bound in confusion. Do we yawn *"Ho-hum"* or do we yell *"Wow!"*? Are our mouths dropping open and our eyes like saucers, or are we blatantly bored with the news that God has come to the region with power and grace?

The crowd concluded that this was jaw-dropping, earthshattering, stop the presses, big time news! The word was out (no matter how much He asked them to remain silent) that God had arrived and done what no other could do. Jesus used His divine touch and saliva to open the ears and loose the tongue of a desperate man. No yawning took place that day. Celebration and adulation were rampant. The God who "does all things well" showed up just in time to make a difference.

Spend time in true hero worship today. Stand amazed at the grace and power of God. Allow yourself to be utterly amazed at His desire to go one-on-one with you. Be blown away by His capabilities and His compassion. No telling what you will *hear* when you listen to His voice through the Scripture, and no telling what you will *say* when you receive what He has to offer. I bet those folks are *still* talking about that day!

Don't Run From the Desolate Place

In those days, when there was again a large crowd and they had nothing to eat, Jesus called His disciples and said to them, "I feel compassion for the people because they have remained with Me now three days and have nothing to eat. If I send them away hungry to their homes, they will faint on the way; and some of them have come from a great distance." And His disciples answered Him, "Where will anyone be able [to find enough] bread here in [this] desolate place to satisfy these people?" And He was asking them, "How many loaves do you have?" And they said, "Seven." And He directed the people to sit down on the ground; and taking the seven loaves, He gave thanks and broke them, and started giving them to His disciples to serve to them, and they served them to the people. They also had a few small fish; and after He had blessed them, He ordered these to be served as well. And they ate and were satisfied; and they picked up seven large baskets full of what was left over of the broken pieces. About four thousand were [there]; and He sent them away. And immediately He entered the boat with His disciples and came to the district of Dalmanutha.

MARK 8:1–10

❧

WE AGAIN FIND Jesus and his friends surrounded by thousands of people who are hungry. We know that their hunger is not, as ours is not, simply a physical hunger. Human hunger is both physical and spiritual. It is the miraculous physical feeding of the multitudes that brings clarity in the understanding of and belief in the true identity of Jesus. He shows Himself to be the Creator who has power to provide. The disciples were still learning that life-changing fact.

The disciples had concluded (even after seeing Him earlier feed the five thousand) that the desolate place they were in was no place to find nourishment. They decided they would never be able to find enough bread there. Seven loaves of bread and a few small fish would not be enough for the thousands of hungry people. They may have believed it was time to run from the desolate place. That would have been true had Jesus not been in that same desolate place. In the hands of the Creator, bread and fish multiply. In the hands of God, "not enough" becomes "more than enough."

Our lives can feel as desolate as the wilderness of the world's driest desert. The spiritual hunger pangs can be as painful as anything we have ever experienced. Fainting along the way is definitely *not* out of the question. But is there enough sustenance in our midst to satisfy the hunger? Can our life be sustained on so little? Only if our desolate place is inhabited by our God. Only if what we have is handed over to the Creator. Left to ourselves and our own resources, our souls will starve.

One of the great lessons of this passage is the lesson of trust. The disciples trusted the power of Christ to do something huge with so little. The disciples handed over what little they had in belief that Jesus could do something big. The reward was a feast for thousands. The reward also was in the joy of seeing people sustained by the nourishment that comes from the hand of God.

Consider what you have right now that compares to seven loaves of bread and a few small fish. So little and yet so useful in the hands of your Creator. Talents that pale in comparison to your neighbor's. Skills that don't measure up in the eyes of the world. Abilities that are naturally imperfect. Resources that are not only limited but also shrinking. Put all of it in the hands of God by faith and watch the Creator use it to advance His Kingdom. Rise up in your desolate place knowing you are standing with your God, and see the thousands nourished by Him. Participate in His feeding of the multitude by believing *so little* can be *so much*. Be ready, also, to pick up baskets of leftovers. For when the Creator provides, He provides more than enough. Remember that it is in the most desolate of places where we see our God offer Divine feasts. Don't run from the desolate place. Dinner is about to be served!

When Is Enough, Enough?

The Pharisees came out and began to argue with Him,
seeking from Him a sign from heaven, to test Him.
Sighing deeply in His spirit, He said, "Why does this
generation seek for a sign? Truly I say to you, no sign
will be given to this generation." Leaving them, He again
embarked and went away to the other side.

MARK 8:11–13

THE PHARISEES MUST have been very threatened as they began to
argue with Jesus. Thousands of people were beginning to use the
title "Messiah" in association with Jesus because of what they had
seen and heard. Thousands were ready to follow Him and this
scared the religious leaders. The argument was over His true identity. *You are not the Messiah so quit acting like it! You are not God so
quit saying you are! If you are who you say you are, show us a sign!* The
Pharisees were testing Him to see if He could produce convincing
evidence. They wanted Him to prove that His authority was truly
from heaven, thus "a sign from heaven."

A "sign" in the Old Testament was seen as evidence that what
was said or done was authentic and could be trusted. It was not
necessarily a demonstration of power. Mark seems to make a dis-
tinction between a sign (the Greek word *semeion*) and a miracle
(the Greek word *dynamis*). The miracles Jesus performed proved
He possessed God's power and presence. Asking for a miracle is
actually not offensive to God. Those requests can be real expres-
sions of faith. Jairus and the Syronphoenician woman (Mark 5 and
7, respectively) are examples of people who asked for miracles out
of their faith in Jesus.

It is one thing to begin a request by saying, "*Because* of who You
are . . ." and quite another to make a demand of God saying, "*If you
are who you say you are* . . ." The Pharisees were demanding some-

thing from Jesus out of a lack of faith. Jesus demonstrated that God does not respond to those kinds of demands. Jesus made it very clear, ". . . no sign will be given . . ."

My question is simple: When is enough, enough? Think of all Jesus had provided them by way of His words and His actions to authenticate His identity. Remember all the miraculous healings and the displays of power as He touched the damaged and ran off the demons. His words were enough to calm storms and His spit was enough to restore speech. Mothers and fathers were given back their children and children were given back their lives. A man who was paralyzed began to walk and a man who lived among the dead began to live among the living.

Jesus once told a similar crowd that the only "sign" they would be given would be the sign of Jonah. This meant they would see Him raised from the dead in three days. What better or bigger sign could someone give to authenticate his claims than to rise from the dead? When is enough, enough?

The sign has been given. It is now time to respond. We can now boldly approach Jesus with all our requests and not our tests. We can begin all our appeals with *Because You are God*, rather than *If you are God*.

Have you heard enough and seen enough? If the resurrection of Jesus Christ is not enough to satisfy someone's doubts then my question remains: when is enough, enough?

His Presence, Person, and Provision

And they had forgotten to take bread, and did not have more than one loaf in the boat with them. And He was giving orders to them, saying, "Watch out! Beware of the leaven of the Pharisees and the leaven of Herod." They [began] to discuss with one another [the fact] that they had no bread. And Jesus, aware of this, said to them, "Why do you discuss [the fact] that you have no bread? Do you not yet see or understand? Do you have a hardened heart? HAVING EYES, DO YOU NOT SEE? AND HAVING EARS, DO YOU NOT HEAR? And do you not remember, when I broke the five loaves for the five thousand, how many baskets full of broken pieces you picked up?" They said to Him, "Twelve." "When [I broke] the seven for the four thousand, how many large baskets full of broken pieces did you pick up?" And they said to Him, "Seven." And He was saying to them, "Do you not yet understand?"

MARK 8:14–21

I DON'T KNOW what it is about us but we tend to forget important life lessons too quickly. Jesus' friends were no different. Just hours after picking up seven baskets of leftover bread, they boarded a boat with only one loaf. By their own admission, they forgot to bring enough bread for the journey. In doing so, they failed to remember some of the more important life lessons taught them by Jesus.

Jesus' warning to them about the "leaven" or "yeast" of the Pharisees and Herod is what sparked the discussion. His mentioning that one particular ingredient opened them up to one of the greatest spiritual life lessons ever: Enjoy God's *presence* while growing close to His *person* and as you enjoy His *provision.*

Let me explain. The lesson for His friends then and now is that in the *presence* of God, one loaf of bread is enough. His promise to all of us is that He will take care of our every need. This gives us the freedom to focus on Him rather than on the problem. The problem for the disciples was that they forgot bread. If they spent too much more time focusing on that one piece of bad news, they would miss the joy of being in the presence of God Himself. A keen awareness of His presence allows us all to admit our errors (failure to appropriate His abundant gifts such as bread) while continuing to trust in His perfection as God.

In focusing in on His perfection as God, we grow close to His *person.* He is the Creator who has chosen to give us life and to lead us to a full experience in that life. He is God and He has chosen to lead us in the journey. He is trustworthy and He is good. Our enemy keeps whispering in our ear that God is not really good. The enemy insists that God cannot be trusted. The truth is, He *is* good and He *can* be trusted.

The last part of the lesson is to trust His *provision.* There is a huge difference between knowledge and understanding. The disciples knew Jesus turned a few loaves of bread and a few small fish into great hillside feasts. What they did not understand, however, is what that really meant. Jesus asked, "Do you not yet understand?"

"Yeast" or "leaven" had become a common metaphor in Jewish culture for any unseen invasive and corrupting influence. Jesus continued to warn his friends about the increasing problem of unbelief that was having a negative influence within the nation of Israel. Unbelief in the *presence, person,* and *provision* of God is the "yeast" or "leaven" of the Pharisees and Herod. They are the ones who did not believe.

There will be many more days for us when we experience the abundant provision of God, and yet we will fail to appropriate that provision, much like the disciples did. There will be many more days when we forget that we are always in the presence of the Almighty God, as did the disciples. My encouragement to us all is that we not forget any of that *today!* We are on a great journey, and it is important that we enjoy His *presence* while we grow close to His *person* as we enjoy His *provision.* Let's not forget any of this!

Watch Out For Walking Trees

And they came to Bethsaida. And they brought a blind
man to Jesus and implored Him to touch him. Taking the
blind man by the hand, He brought him out of the village;
and after spitting on his eyes and laying His hands on him,
He asked him, "Do you see anything?" And he looked up
and said, "I see men, for I see [them] like trees, walking
around." Then again He laid His hands on his eyes; and
he looked intently and was restored, and [began] to see
everything clearly. And He sent him to his home, saying,
"Do not even enter the village."

MARK 8:22–26

THE MIRACLE IN this passage is very similar to the one in which
Jesus took the deaf and mute man away from the crowd and used
His spit in the process of healing (Mark 7). This time, Jesus took
the hand of a blind man and led him out of the village. Jesus used
His spit and His touch to give sight to the man. There is an inter-
esting detail to this story that we must not overlook.

The detail has to do with *progress*. Notice that when the man's
vision was restored and he was asked if he saw anything, his response was, "I see men, for I see them like trees, walking around."
Jesus then laid His hands on Him again, and the man began to see
everything clearly. Progress is a very beautiful and normal thing in
our journeys of faith.

Our one-on-one relationships with Jesus grow as we are moved
further away from the opinions and influences of the crowd. Jesus
demonstrated a desire to be alone with this blind man and would
want us to know He has the same desire for us. Taking us by the
hand and leading us away from the crowd gives us the alone time
we need with Him. It is in these intimate encounters that progress
takes place.

This encounter is a great picture of what was happening in the hearts of Jesus' disciples as well as what continues to happen in our own hearts. Jesus' friends were challenged in the boat to consider the fact that even though they had ears and eyes, they were having trouble "hearing" and "seeing." Our spiritual vision is blurry now but will one day be made perfect. We may definitely have faith in Christ, but we still struggle to see clearly. In the passage, when Jesus touches the man again, it is then that his sight becomes perfect. Paul told the Corinthians and us that, "For now we see in a mirror dimly, but then face to face; now I know in part, but then I will know fully just as I also have been fully known" (1 Corinthians 13:12).

There are several things about the passage in Mark that grip my heart. First of all, Jesus took the man by the hand and led Him to a place where they could be alone. Secondly, Jesus touched Him with His hands and with His saliva. This very intimate contact communicated God's desire to be close to the people He created in love. It communicated His power to make a difference physically and spiritually. I am also gripped by the fact that Jesus allowed this man to be in process. The hope we are given is that one day we will see perfectly. Until we see perfectly in heaven, life on earth will be an adventure of living among "walking trees." This means life will not always make sense. This means we will continue to walk by faith in the presence of our God. It means we won't have perfect understanding. It means we will be in a process that leads to progress.

Allow Jesus to "take you by the hand" today and lead you to a place where you can be alone with Him. Don't let the roar and the draw of the crowd keep you from being alone with Christ. Let me also encourage you to trust the power of God as you enjoy intimacy with Him. His desire to be close and His ability to heal are to be enjoyed and utilized by us all. Lastly, settle into the journey and realize it is a process that leads to progress. Be encouraged, we will one day "see" perfectly. Until then, watch out for walking trees!

It's Personal

Jesus went out, along with His disciples, to the villages
of Caesarea Philippi; and on the way He questioned His
disciples, saying to them, "Who do people say that I am?"
They told Him, saying, "John the Baptist; and others
[say] Elijah; but others, one of the prophets." And He
[continued] by questioning them, "But who do you say
that I am?" Peter answered and said to Him, "You are the
Christ." And He warned them to tell no one about Him.

MARK 8:27–30

❧

AS JESUS CONTINUED to travel with His friends on their way to
Caesarea Philippi, the conversation turned to His identity. The
general population had not yet come to know His true identity as
evidenced by their answers to the question, "Who do people say
that I am?" If Jesus was not John the Baptist, Elijah, or one of the
prophets, then who was He?

Everything Jesus had said and done up to this point was leading to Peter's climactic confession. Mark has brought us halfway
through this good news account in order to show us that Jesus was
the Christ. He has given us a very detailed account of His words
and works to show that He *was* the Messiah. The question now is
whether folks like you and me believe Him.

People today are really no different than those who lived during the time of Christ. People today have certain ideas about Jesus
and those ideas carry certain expectations. We, like the disciples,
are learning as we go. Notice that there are two questions for the
disciples to answer. The first one has to do with who the *people*
say Jesus is, and the second one has to do with who *they* say He is.
The first question may not have been too threatening, whereas the
second question may have been very threatening. The second question made it very personal. His asking them, "Who do *you* say that

I am?" (emphasis added) tells us that individuals must answer for themselves. What others say about Jesus does not ultimately matter when it comes to our personal relationship with Jesus. We must answer the question for ourselves.

When did you first answer that question for yourself? When did it get personal? Remember that when it comes to you and Jesus, it does not matter how your aunts, uncles, cousins, neighbors, mailman, or dry cleaner answer that question. When it comes to your relationship with God, it does not matter how your mom or dad answers the question nor how your children answer the question. Jesus is asking each one of us personally, *Who do* you *say that I am?*

Everyone needs a Messiah. Everyone has been separated from God by his or her sin, and so everyone needs to be rescued. Jesus came to "seek and to save" all of us. Therefore, all of us must decide if we believe He is able to rescue.

Neither John the Baptist, Elijah, nor any of the prophets pointed to themselves as being able to rescue people from their brokenness. Only Jesus pointed to Himself. This means we must trust only Jesus. I hope you find it encouraging that Jesus cares what *your* answer is. He is a personal God who has personally sought you out for a relationship. He knows there is no other way back to the Father but through Him, so He wants to know your answer. Forget, for a moment, what others believe about Jesus and allow His question to hit home with you. To worry about what others say about Jesus is to depersonalize the issue. Remember that when it comes to you and Jesus . . . it's personal!

Champion or Chump?

And He began to teach them that the Son of Man must
suffer many things and be rejected by the elders and the
chief priests and the scribes, and be killed, and after three
days rise again. And He was stating the matter plainly.
And Peter took Him aside and began to rebuke Him. But
turning around and seeing His disciples, He rebuked Peter
and said, "Get behind Me, Satan; for you are not setting
your mind on God's interests, but man's."

MARK 8:31–33

AS THE SPOKESMAN for the disciples, Peter became the champion
when he boldly confessed that Jesus was the Christ. They were
convinced (all but one, that is) that the words and works of Jesus
proved He was who He said He was. The first part of Mark's gospel
led up to that climactic confession of faith, "You are the Christ."
While the first part of Mark's good news account shows us that He
was the Messiah, the second part of his gospel shows us what *kind*
of Messiah (suffering rather than conquering) Jesus was going to
be.

The expectation from the Jewish nation in the days of Christ
was that the Messiah would arrive as a conqueror of Rome. Their
expectations were for the Christ to free them from the political tyranny of an occupying force. Jesus, however, revealed to His disciples
that He was a different kind of Messiah. Because the disciples did
not yet know the whole story regarding Jesus as a suffering Messiah,
they were forbidden from sharing what they did know. Jesus, however, was going to bring them up to speed.

Jesus plainly told them that He would suffer many things, be
rejected by the spiritual leadership of Israel, be killed, and yet rise
from the dead three days later. Apart from the news of the resurrection, the message He delivered to His friends may have been equiv-

alent to a sucker punch to the gut. That is *not* what they wanted to hear. That is *not* what they thought they needed. Is it any surprise that Peter stepped in with his bold objection to Jesus' death? Based on Jesus' response, we see that Peter quickly went from being the *champion* to being the *chump*.

The difference between being a champion and a chump is simple. To have our minds set on God's interests is to be a champion and to have our minds set on man's interests is to be a chump. Now, if it sounds harsh to you for me to use the word "chump," let's keep in mind the word Christ used for Peter . . . *Satan*. Remember that Satan did not want Jesus to go to the cross. Satan somehow knew that if Jesus were to die a substitutionary death for people, his attempts to keep them separated from God would be hindered. It was in the wilderness that he tempted Jesus to rule the nations without going to the cross.

While man's interests would be to have Jesus ride into town on a white horse to save us from physical tyranny, God's interests would be to rescue us from spiritual tyranny. Peter was not willing to accept that spiritual liberation was to come through the cross.

Will we be champions or chumps today? Will we have our minds set on our interests or on God's interests? To approach God with our agenda in mind is to approach God in the flesh. To approach God with His agenda in mind is to approach Him in the Spirit. The former approach gets in the way of spiritual progress while the latter approach does the opposite. The former way is to be a *chump* while the latter is to be a *champion*.

If we were to ask ourselves what we *really* want, we would all admit that we want to be champions. No one *really* wants to be a chump. Therefore, let's set our minds on the interests of God. Let's remember, however, that this will take us to the cross. If we are ready for the cross then we are ready to be the champion!

Following Jesus Is Hard

And He summoned the crowd with His disciples, and said
to them, "If anyone wishes to come after Me, he must deny
himself, and take up his cross and follow Me. For whoever
wishes to save his life will lose it, but whoever loses his
life for My sake and the gospel's will save it. For what does
it profit a man to gain the whole world, and forfeit his
soul? For what will a man give in exchange for his soul?
For whoever is ashamed of Me and My words in this
adulterous and sinful generation, the Son of Man will also
be ashamed of him when He comes in the glory of His
Father with the holy angels."

MARK 8:34–38

IF YOU THINK it was hard for the disciples to hear Jesus say He
was going to be rejected and killed, just imagine the terror they
felt as He called for them to pick up their own cross and get in
line. Imagine the shock of hearing they were asked to lose their life.
They may have wondered why Jesus, all of a sudden, began talking about death. Why spoil things with talk of losing life, denying
self, forfeiting souls, being an adulterous and sinful generation, and
possibly being ashamed? The reason is simple . . . Jesus was serious
about His friends experiencing life to its fullest measure.

The disciples were about to learn one very difficult lesson: following Jesus was going to be hard. The requirements for discipleship were stringent. Denying self, carrying a cross, and losing their
life definitely "raised the bar" for the disciples.

What may have sounded like a riddle was really a road map.
What may have sounded like a confusing puzzle was really the
Creator's plan for abundant living. Jesus was promising to provide
eternal life that would begin in the "here and now," and self-denial
was the beginning of that journey. The crowd Jesus was address-

ing that day found out that experiencing the abundant life would include some difficult choices.

But what does it mean to deny self? What does it mean to carry our cross? What did Jesus mean when He said that if someone wishes to save his life he must lose it? We must consider these things to be a Divine call to abandon our own efforts and rely totally on Jesus. Just as dead bodies do not dig themselves out of graves, you and I do not dig ourselves out of the pit of spiritual death. In the time of Christ, crosses were used to bring about death. Jesus takes us to that *terrifying* place to show us that the *terrific* life we seek can be found only in line with Him.

The suffering Messiah calls followers to get in line with Him. Do you see why I say following Jesus is hard? We instinctively want to save our lives. Our flesh does not want to suffer. Our flesh runs from suffering at every opportunity. Jesus, however, calls us to deny self, take up our cross, and follow Him at every opportunity.

Consider what we gain by believing and obeying Jesus in this. We live *rescued* lives. We are lifted from the pit of everyday "here and now" spiritual death. We live *exchanged* lives. Jesus has taken our old life and exchanged it for His. Since we had nothing to give in exchange for our souls, Jesus did it for us. We live *unashamed* lives. We not only stand before our family and friends with news of our loyalty to Jesus, but Jesus stands before His Father and angels with news of His loyalty to us.

Yes, following Jesus is hard. But following Jesus also leads to rescued lives, exchanged lives, and lives that are unashamed. If this sounds good to you . . . then get in line!

Jesus Stands Alone

And Jesus was saying to them, "Truly I say to you, there are some of those who are standing here who will not taste death until they see the kingdom of God after it has come with power."

Six days later, Jesus took with Him Peter and James and John, and brought them up on a high mountain by themselves. And He was transfigured before them; and His garments became radiant and exceedingly white, as no launderer on earth can whiten them. Elijah appeared to them along with Moses; and they were talking with Jesus. Peter said to Jesus, "Rabbi, it is good for us to be here; let us make three tabernacles, one for You, and one for Moses, and one for Elijah." For he did not know what to answer; for they became terrified. Then a cloud formed, overshadowing them, and a voice came out of the cloud, "This is My beloved Son, listen to Him!" All at once they looked around and saw no one with them anymore, except Jesus alone.

MARK 9:1–8

JESUS PROMISED SOME of His friends that they would not taste the sting of death until they saw the power of God's coming kingdom. I would imagine this was a very welcomed promise since the painful news of Jesus' suffering and death was still being felt. I am convinced that what they saw and heard on the mountain that day forever changed the way they saw Jesus.

Seeing Jesus temporarily changed into His glorified body and standing in the presence of Moses and Elijah made Peter want to settle in on the mountain. Peter, not knowing what to say, simply stated the obvious, "Rabbi, it is good for us to be here ..." The bold and impetuous Peter wanted to do more than talk about the greatness of the moment. He wanted to build shelters for the three great men he saw. He wanted construction to begin immediately. He wanted one shelter for Moses, the great liberator; one shelter for Elijah, the great prophet; and one shelter for Jesus, the great teacher. At this point in Peter's life, all three men were equal. In Peter's heart, Jesus was standing among peers. He and his friends, however, were about to learn the truth.

From out of the overshadowing cloud came the authoritative voice of the God of the universe. God met them all on the mountain that day to set the record straight about who Jesus really was. God clearly communicated, "This is My beloved Son, listen to Him!" In the original Greek, the second part of that sentence literally means, "obey Him!" This makes it very clear. Jesus was not standing among peers. Jesus was clearly introduced as the beloved Son of God.

While Moses was the giver of the Law, Jesus *fulfilled* the Law. While Moses was the liberator of a nation, Jesus was the liberator of the *world*. While the prophets communicated the Word of God, Jesus *was* the Word of God. Once the cloud disappeared, the disciples saw that Jesus literally stood alone. The message was clear and concise: Jesus was and is greater than Moses and greater than all the prophets.

Does Jesus stand alone in your life, or do you consider Jesus to be just another great teacher among great teachers? Who are you listening to and obeying in life? Remember the clear and concise message that was heard on the mountain that day, "This is My beloved Son, listen to Him!" Jesus, the Messiah, must stand alone as our liberator. Jesus, the Word of God, must stand alone as our authority. There is no one equal to Him.

Let's not see Jesus standing among peers. There are some great people in history, but none greater than Jesus. There are some great teachers today, but none greater than Christ. There are great liberators all around, but none greater than the Lord. Keep in mind what God declared on the mountain that day, "This is My beloved Son, listen to Him!" According to the Father, Jesus stands alone. Let's live our lives like we believe that.

When We Still Have Questions

As they were coming down from the mountain, He gave them orders not to relate to anyone what they had seen, until the Son of Man rose from the dead. They seized upon that statement, discussing with one another what rising from the dead meant. They asked Him, saying, "[Why is it] that the scribes say that Elijah must come first?" And He said to them, "Elijah does first come and restore all things. And [yet] how is it written of the Son of Man that He will suffer many things and be treated with contempt? "But I say to you that Elijah has indeed come, and they did to him whatever they wished, just as it is written of him."

MARK 9:9–13

THINGS WERE SO clear on the mountain. The disciples got the message and were thrilled to hear from God. While Peter and his friends may have wanted to stay on the mountain for the rest of their lives, Jesus would not allow it. Things may have seemed very clear on the mountain since they all heard directly from God, but they had to descend into the valley. It was on the mountain that they got the very clear and concise message that Jesus was to stand alone in their hearts and souls, and they were all ready to live out that truth. So then how did things get so confusing so quickly?

Imagine how confusing it was to receive strict orders to remain silent about what they had seen. In addition to that, there was much confusion about what it meant for Jesus to rise from the dead. But wait, there's more! There was confusion about the return of Elijah to "restore all things." There was confusion about the Son of Man having to suffer many things and be treated with contempt. So, what do we do with all this confusion? Wouldn't you have thought that hearing straight from God would have cleared the water rather than have muddied it? If only it were so!

Jesus graciously provided some help in this by *not* providing help. In other words, Jesus aided His friends in their journey of faith by allowing them to wrestle with their questions . . . for a time. There is something very encouraging for me in seeing the disciples struggle with their questions and realizing Jesus did not run to the rescue with ironclad answers. As a matter of fact, instead of giving any answer at all, we see that Jesus actually answered their question with a question as they walked down the mountain. Even in their confusion, they walked with Jesus.

I am finding that the longer I walk with Jesus on my own journey of faith, the more comfortable I become with the times when I still have questions. I am finding I am not as anxious when things get a bit confusing. I believe I have grown in this area mostly because of all the other experiences I have had when the Lord was *very* clear with me. The disciples were coming off a wonderful "mountaintop" encounter with God. The message they received from Him was extremely clear and concise. This encounter with God allowed them, I believe, to continue on even in the midst of many unanswered questions.

How are you doing in this area of your journey? Are there lots of questions about what *this* or *that* means? Are there questions about God's timing? Do you find yourself wondering what Jesus is up to in your life? If so, you are not alone. One thing to keep in mind as you journey with Him is that the answers *will* one day come. For the disciples, the resurrection brought clarity to the transfiguration, as the command to remain silent turned into a command to tell the world. Jesus gave clear direction to them regarding John the Baptist filling the role of Elijah. Jesus continued to assure them that though He be rejected and killed, He would rise from the dead to conquer sin. I have found that the resurrection is what brings me peace when I still have lots of unanswered questions!

What happens when we still have questions? I say we keep walking with Jesus and looking forward to the day when we will walk with Him in heaven. I am sure eternity will afford us a lot of time for questions and answers.

Spiritual Roadblocks

When they came [back] to the disciples, they saw a large crowd around them, and [some] scribes arguing with them. Immediately, when the entire crowd saw Him, they were amazed and [began] running up to greet Him. And He asked them, "What are you discussing with them?" And one of the crowd answered Him, "Teacher, I brought You my son, possessed with a spirit which makes him mute; and whenever it seizes him, it slams him [to the ground] and he foams [at the mouth], and grinds his teeth and stiffens out. I told Your disciples to cast it out, and they could not [do it]." And He answered them and said, "O unbelieving generation, how long shall I be with you? How long shall I put up with you? Bring him to Me!" They brought the boy to Him. When he saw Him, immediately the spirit threw him into a convulsion, and falling to the ground, he [began] rolling around and foaming [at the mouth]. And He asked his father, "How long has this been happening to him?" And he said, "From childhood. It has often thrown him both into the fire and into the water to destroy him. But if You can do anything, take pity on us and help us!" And Jesus said to him, "'If You can?' All things are possible to him who believes." Immediately the boy's father cried out and said, "I do believe; help my unbelief." When Jesus saw that a crowd was rapidly gathering, He rebuked the unclean spirit, saying to it, "You deaf and mute spirit, I command you, come out of him and do not enter him again." After crying out and throwing him into terrible convulsions, it came out; and [the boy] became so much like a corpse that most [of them] said, "He is dead!" But Jesus took him by the hand and raised him; and he got up. When He came into [the] house, His disciples [began] questioning Him privately, "Why could we not drive it out?" And He said to them, "This kind cannot come out by anything but prayer."

MARK 9:14–29

JESUS AND HIS three traveling companions came down from the mountain to find the rest of the disciples facing a spiritual roadblock. They walked down from the mountain to find His followers embroiled in controversy. Even though some of the scribes were arguing with the disciples, we are never told exactly what they were arguing about. We do know, however, that the disciples had hit a spiritual roadblock, as they were unable to overcome the deaf and mute demon that had gripped a father's dear son.

The event seems to be in stark contrast to the power and glory just seen and experienced by the three disciples who walked up the mountain with Jesus. It seems that we are to live our lives in the dependent presence of Jesus. It seems that when we try to live our lives independent of Jesus' power and glory, we face spiritual roadblocks that impede our progress.

Consider all the years of agony the father and son experienced as they battled the demon that not only kept the son from hearing and speaking, but continually tried to destroy the boy by throwing him into scorching fires and deep waters. Apart from Christ, the road to that spiritual freedom and security would remain blocked.

Consider the inability on the disciples' part to deal with the demon. Apart from Christ, they failed to win the spiritual battle. Without the power of Jesus, the road to spiritual victory would remain hopelessly blocked.

The demon in question was apparently a certain kind. Jesus said, "This kind cannot come out by anything but prayer." This particular kind of demon had taken control of the boy when he was young and was holding on to him with great determination. Even as Jesus confronted the demon, the struggle turned violent. The result of the battle appeared to end in death, but the actual result was a life restored. The spiritual battle facing the disciples, the father, and the tormented son was about faith and trust in the power of Jesus to restore life.

The father, learning that the disciples had no power of their own, said to Jesus, "But if you can do anything, take pity on us and help us!" Jesus used the father's own words to show that all things are possible for those who believe. Jesus turned things around on the father by putting the "if" back on him. Clearly, the issue was if the father could believe and trust in the power of Jesus to remove the roadblock.

Consider the spiritual roadblocks you face today. Is there a certain sin that controls you? Are you being confronted by people who love to argue against your faith? Have you been living your life apart from a desperate dependence on Jesus? If so, remember that Jesus has said that all things (even defeating spiritual roadblocks) are possible to him who believes. Prayer is the privilege given to God's friends by which they not only express their trust and hope in His power, but by which they are able to move His compassionate hand in the removal of spiritual roadblocks. Jesus Himself said, "All things are possible to him who believes." If that statement in itself is a roadblock for you, pray about it and see what happens!

They Were Afraid To Ask

From there they went out and [began] to go through Galilee, and He did not want anyone to know [about it]. For He was teaching His disciples and telling them, "The Son of Man is to be delivered into the hands of men, and they will kill Him; and when He has been killed, He will rise three days later." But they did not understand [this] statement, and they were afraid to ask Him.

MARK 9:30–32

JESUS TRAVELED CAREFULLY through Galilee so as not to be recognized by the crowds. He wanted some uninterrupted time with His disciples as He prepared them for what was about to happen. He wanted plenty of time for questions and answers. They were on a difficult journey toward the crucifixion of Christ, and there were bound to be questions.

Jesus was blunt with His teaching when He said, "The Son of Man is to be delivered into the hands of men, and they will kill Him; and when He has been killed, He will rise three days later." Though they did not understand His statement, they were afraid to ask Him any questions. It does not say they did not have any questions, but rather they were afraid to ask Him questions.

I can only imagine what questions they may have had. *Delivered? By whom? Into the hands of men? Which men? Kill Him? Why? Rise three days later? How?* So many questions and yet so little courage to ask. So little understanding, yet so much fear. What were they afraid of? Why not ask questions of the Teacher?

Could it be that because they failed to defeat the deaf and mute demon with the *power* of Jesus, they did not want to also admit failure to understand the *teaching* of Jesus? Could it be they were afraid Jesus was losing His patience with them? Was He speaking of them when He asked earlier, "How long shall I put up with you?"

Maybe failing to understand spiritual truth just after failing to win the spiritual battle was too difficult for them to admit. Rather than ask questions, they may have nodded with a polite smile and acted like they knew what He was talking about.

What are you doing with your questions? Are you stuffing them behind a polite smile in fear that God is losing His patience with you? Have you experienced so many failures in life that you are unwilling to admit to God you fail to understand His plan? If so, let me encourage you to fear not.

The journey to the cross was a difficult journey for Jesus and His friends. Jesus was preparing them at a pace they could handle, knowing that it would take time for them to embrace a *suffering* Messiah rather than a *conquering* One. He knew it would take time for them to understand it would be one of *them* who would deliver Him to the authorities; it would be religious leaders in cahoots with political leaders who would destroy Him. They would later come to realize that Jesus' death was divinely mandated for the forgiveness of their sins. Time would be needed for them to realize that the same power of God that defeated demons would be the power that would defeat death.

I can't help but wonder if their pace toward understanding would have picked up had they not been afraid to ask Jesus more questions. I can't help but think that their acceptance of a suffering Messiah would have been easier had they not stuffed their questions behind a polite smile and a simple nod. Let's not be afraid to ask God for understanding. Let's not stuff our questions behind a polite smile. If God is big and powerful enough to raise the dead to life, He is certainly big and powerful enough to handle our questions. A difficult journey will bring about difficult questions. Let's not be afraid to ask questions along the way.

Service Over Status

They came to Capernaum; and when He was in the house,
He [began] to question them, "What were you discussing
on the way?" But they kept silent, for on the way they
had discussed with one another which [of them was] the
greatest. Sitting down, He called the twelve and said to
them, "If anyone wants to be first, he shall be last of all
and servant of all." Taking a child, He set him before them,
and taking him in His arms, He said to them, "Whoever
receives one child like this in My name receives Me; and
whoever receives Me does not receive Me, but Him who
sent Me."

MARK 9:33–37

As JESUS AND His disciples settled in at a home in Capernaum,
Jesus asked them a very direct question about the discussion they
had been having on the way. The discussion or argument had been
about who was the greatest.

It seems that as the messianic kingdom approached, the twelve
friends of Jesus were positioning themselves for rank. It may
have been that the extra attention given to Peter, James, and John
sparked the discussion of status. Their silence in response to Jesus'
point-blank question may have been a sign of their embarrassment
in the matter.

The silence of the disciples provided a tremendous opportunity
for Jesus to teach an important lesson about *service* over *status* in
God's kingdom. As Jesus sat down (the customary position of an
authoritative teacher), He did not scold them for their desire to
be first nor for their desire to be great. Rather than scolding the
disciples, Jesus shared with them the connection between being last
in God's kingdom and being first. To be "first" in the kingdom, one
would have to be last.

Jesus used a living illustration as He put a child in front of them. Embracing the child in His arms, Jesus told of receiving the child in His name. In a culture that held the mature adult in such high esteem, the graphic display of embracing the child and equating that embrace with the receiving of Christ and His Father surely caught their attention. In biblical times, the child was seen as the least significant person in Jewish society. Jesus was saying to His disciples that to have true status in the kingdom, one must be a servant.

How are you doing in the area of serving others? If you are like me, you would have to admit that status matters to some degree. How people view us tends to be important. I would imagine if we had been on the road to Capernaum that day, you and I would have had the same argument the disciples had.

Imagine the difference it would make in your home if the argument after dinner was between folks who *wanted* to do the dishes. Just think how different it would be at work if people started *serving* one another instead of *stepping* on one another. Picture the changes that would take place in your neighborhood if the least significant person was embraced by others.

The messianic kingdom was ushered in by the suffering Messiah. He Himself became the least in order to rescue the world. Jesus took on the role of a servant from the day He was born until the day He died in order to lead the way for the rest of us. Desiring to be great in the kingdom of God is not bad. What is bad is when we choose *status* over *service*. The kingdom of God is about service to all rather than status above all. To be at the front of the line, we must put ourselves at the end of the line. I have decided that if that spot was good enough for Jesus, it will be just fine for me.

Do Not Hinder

John said to Him, "Teacher, we saw someone casting
out demons in Your name, and we tried to prevent him
because he was not following us." But Jesus said, "Do not
hinder him, for there is no one who will perform a miracle
in My name, and be able soon afterward to speak evil of
Me. For he who is not against us is for us. For whoever
gives you a cup of water to drink because of your name as
[followers] of Christ, truly I say to you, he will not lose his
reward."

MARK 9:38–41

JOHN BROUGHT TO Jesus' attention the fact that someone was casting out demons in His name. It was someone who was not following them. It was someone who looked to be working alone. The assumption on John's part was that Jesus would want that person stopped . . . but the assumption was wrong.

What would possibly drive John and his friends to want to hinder someone from fighting spiritual battles in the name of Jesus? What forces were at work in their own spirits that would cause them to be uncomfortable with the work of this lone warrior?

It could have been *fear* that motivated them to bring the issue to Christ. Fear could have certainly stepped in to say, *Watch out, you are not the only exorcist in town!* Fear could certainly motivate people to keep the competition out. Fear of not being the only ones to enjoy the pleasure of the Lord as they worked to advance the Kingdom could have motivated them to hinder this spiritual soldier. It could have been *jealousy*. Jealousy certainly could have stepped in to say, *Watch out, you are not the* best *exorcist in town!* It was not long before this that the disciples had failed to cast out a demon. Word on the street was that this particular person was casting out demons (note the plural)! Jealousy has a way of rearing its ugly head when others succeed while we fail.

Jesus sought to calm those fears and jealousies by assuring His friends that folks who are fighting spiritual battles in the name of Christ, even though they are fighting on a different front, must not be hindered. Any work done in the name of Christ is worthy of reward. A simple cup of cool water, given in the name of Christ, is noticed and rewarded by the Lord.

Have you and I settled in to a certain way of doing ministry? Have we begun to look at the churches and ministries down the street with fear and jealousy? Have we become prideful over the method of our work for Christ? It can become easy for us to settle in to a certain way of doing ministry and then boldly title it "God's way." Somehow we allow ourselves to believe that anyone who is not doing ministry "God's way" must be wrong, and thus stopped.

Fear, jealousy, and pride can motivate us to hinder the spiritual work of great "foot soldiers" rather than rally around them with encouragement to fight on. We must recognize that there are thousands of churches and ministries around us that do ministry a bit differently than we do, but are working in the name and power of Christ. These faithful warriors are relieving spiritual oppression. These faithful foot soldiers are offering cool cups of water to those who need spiritual refreshment, and their work is pleasing to God.

There are plenty of folks doing ministry in plenty of different ways. Let's make a list of churches and ministries that are working in the name and power of Christ, and begin praying for them. Jesus has told us not to hinder the work of these ministries.

Radical Demands

"Whoever causes one of these little ones who believe
to stumble, it would be better for him if, with a heavy
millstone hung around his neck, he had been cast into
the sea. If your hand causes you to stumble, cut it off; it is
better for you to enter life crippled, than, having your two
hands, to go into hell, into the unquenchable fire, [where
THEIR WORM DOES NOT DIE, AND THE FIRE IS NOT
QUENCHED]. If your foot causes you to stumble, cut it off;
it is better for you to enter life lame, than, having your two
feet, to be cast into hell, [where THEIR WORM DOES NOT
DIE, AND THE FIRE IS NOT QUENCHED]. If your eye causes
you to stumble, throw it out; it is better for you to enter
the kingdom of God with one eye, than, having two eyes,
to be cast into hell, where THEIR WORM DOES NOT DIE,
AND THE FIRE IS NOT QUENCHED."

MARK 9:42–48

THESE VERSES DO not generate too many warm and fuzzy feelings
in me. I do find these verses difficult, yet very necessary for my walk
with Christ. As you can tell, desperate warnings, devastating consequences, deadly results, and radical demands in relation to the
snare of sin dominate today's passage. Jesus chose to lay it on the
line for His friends in the area of the consequences of deliberately
leading a young believer astray, as well as allowing *themselves* to be
led astray.

Jesus first warned His friends not to hinder people who were
doing ministry in His name. The undeveloped faith of that one
lone exorcist must be encouraged rather than discouraged. He then
warned them about the severe consequences for the person who
would deliberately lead a young believer into sin, as well as move
into sin himself.

Discipleship definitely brings with it some radical demands. Jesus emphasized the demands of following Him by using several hyperboles. He said that whenever the work of "your hand" (the outward tool used to build on inward inclinations) causes you to sin, cut it off. Jesus calls us to take quick and decisive action against all the things that would entice us to fall away. Just as doctors were quick to amputate diseased limbs so that the person who suffered from gangrene would not die, we are to be as skillful and decisive when it comes to the sin in our lives. Because temptations come to us in various ways, Jesus' hyperbole also included the "foot" and the "eye."

To cut off a hand or a foot would take real determination on the part of the one who would take seriously the call to follow Jesus. To be willing to pluck out an eye shows genuine commitment to the cause. Knowing that those who do not put their faith in Christ face a tormented future in a place Jesus called hell should indicate to us the fierce hatred God has for sin. The intensity of that same warning should also indicate to us the amazing love He has for the sinner.

Consider what drastic steps you may need to take in light of what tempts you to fall away from Christ. What lures you away from Him? Impure thoughts, inappropriate interactions, out of control living, addictions, and selfishness pull us all away from our Lord. Let's take the radical demands of discipleship seriously. Let's be ready to perform the difficult surgery needed to enjoy our relationships with Jesus. Just as Jesus warned against deliberately leading a young believer astray, He warned us to be careful not to let ourselves be led astray. The demands sound radical but the rewards, we are assured, are worth it.

Please Pass The Salt

"For everyone will be salted with fire. Salt is good; but if the salt becomes unsalty, with what will you make it salty [again]? Have salt in yourselves, and be at peace with one another."

MARK 9:49–50

❦

MUCH TO MY doctor's dismay, the first words I usually utter at the dinner table after the blessing are, "Please pass the salt." I am terrible about salting my food even before I taste it. I have given it some thought as to why I do that, and all I can come up with is that I really like the taste of salt. I don't mean to insult the chef, but I really do like what salt does for my dining experience.

Jesus ended His teaching moment with His disciples (which included His words about service over status) with important words about salt, my favorite condiment. In those days, people got their salt from the area just to the southwest of the Dead Sea. The salt that was gathered from that site was coarse and impure. It would lose its saltiness over time, but would still have the appearance of salt-like crystals. Jesus took this condiment and preservative to make a concluding point about life.

Jesus said, "For everyone will be salted with fire." I believe that when He said "everyone," He meant what He said. I believe He had in mind both the *believer* and the *unbeliever* when He said "everyone." The unbeliever will be salted with the preserving or continuing fire of hell's ultimate judgment. Jesus often warned people of the torment of hell. As a matter of fact, Jesus mentioned hell more than He mentioned heaven. By mentioning being "salted with fire," Jesus was warning of the horrible consequence of rejecting His grace.

The believer, however, will be salted with the refining fire of life's bitter and painful trials. The suffering that accompanies life will be the refining fire Jesus had in mind. Just as fire is used to burn off the impurities of gold and silver, trials will be used by God to purify and flavor the lives of His people.

We are to have that "salt" in our lives. Our loyalty to Jesus must be steady at all costs. Being "salted with fire" is what purges the impurities from within us. We are not to lose that saltiness. We are to maintain it by staying loyal to Christ. The first command given by the Lord in this passage is to "have salt in yourselves." The second command given by the Lord in this passage is to "be at peace with one another." It seems that the two commands are tied together. If we remain loyal to Christ and not run from the refining fire, we will be able to maintain great relationships with one another. There will be no struggles for status as we choose to serve one another in peace.

Everyone will be salted with fire. Those who are separated from Christ will feel the preserving fire of hell while those who have trusted Him for forgiveness will experience the refining fire that purges the impurities. Let's take some time to chew on the truth contained in today's passage. While you chew on this passage, would you do me a favor? Would you please pass me the salt?

Jesus And Divorce

Getting up, He went from there to the region of Judea and beyond the Jordan; crowds gathered around Him again, and, according to His custom, He once more [began] to teach them.

[Some] Pharisees came up to Jesus, testing Him, and [began] to question Him whether it was lawful for a man to divorce a wife. And He answered and said to them, "What did Moses command you?" They said, "Moses permitted [a man] TO WRITE A CERTIFICATE OF DIVORCE AND SEND [her] AWAY." But Jesus said to them, "Because of your hardness of heart he wrote you this commandment. But from the beginning of creation, [God] MADE THEM MALE AND FEMALE. FOR THIS REASON A MAN SHALL LEAVE HIS FATHER AND MOTHER, AND THE TWO SHALL BECOME ONE FLESH; so they are no longer two, but one flesh. What therefore God has joined together, let no man separate."

In the house the disciples [began] questioning Him about this again. And He said to them, "Whoever divorces his wife and marries another woman commits adultery against her; and if she herself divorces her husband and marries another man, she is committing adultery."

MARK 10:1–12

❧

WHILE TEACHING A large crowd in Judea, Jesus was interrupted by a group of Pharisees who were wanting to test Him. Their ultimate goal was to bring Jesus up on charges, and their thinking was that if they could trap Him into expressing something contrary to Moses and the Jewish law, then charges could be filed.

The subject matter they chose as the bait for the trap was the very painful and difficult topic of divorce. Divorce is an issue that has a tremendous amount of emotional, spiritual, and sometimes physical damage associated with it. Divorce communicates things to people that God never intended to be communicated. The breakup of a marriage oftentimes indicates and communicates rejection, unfaithfulness, deceitfulness, hatred, bitterness, fear, and hopelessness.

It is too bad those religious thugs trivialized the tragedy of divorce by making it the bait for their trap. It is too bad they *schemed* rather than *grieved* in regards to divorce. It is in the midst of seeing some religious ruffians trying to trap Jesus that we see the heart of God revealed when it comes to the sanctity of marriage. Divorce not only interrupts the perfect will of God, but it destroys His perfect design for what is meant to be the most safe and secure place to be human . . . a marriage.

A marriage is meant to be a place to live out unconditional love. It is a place to learn what it is to give rather than take. It is designed to be a safe place to develop trust as we learn to develop vulnerability. It is where we learn what love can really be. Love is when someone knows you well enough to destroy you and chooses not to. "Two becoming one flesh" is not just a nice concept to be considered. It is not just something we say at weddings, among all the other stuff we say at weddings, while we wait for the cake to be cut. "Two becoming one flesh" is God's design for the people He desperately loves. Marriage is a living and breathing picture of how He and His Church are intimately and permanently connected.

Jesus makes it very clear that marriage was designed to be *intimate* and *permanent*. This is why divorce grieves the very heart of God. Divorce, we are told by Christ, is a direct result of hardened hearts. Soft hearts are loving, caring, forgiving, listening, friendly, believing, and tender. Soft hearts develop only as they beat in unison with God's heart and are designed to beat in unison in the safety and sanctity of a marriage between a man and woman. It is when those hearts harden that divorce ravages the home.

For those who *have not* fallen in this area, the work to develop soft and pliable hearts must continue so as not to fall. For those who *have* fallen in this area or who have been burned by the abandonment of a spouse whose heart was hardened, they must find their place in the forgiving and healing heart of God. It is God's heart that never hardens but is always tender.

A Childlike Faith

And they were bringing children to Him so that He might touch them; but the disciples rebuked them. But when Jesus saw this, He was indignant and said to them, "Permit the children to come to Me; do not hinder them; for the kingdom of God belongs to such as these. Truly I say to you, whoever does not receive the kingdom of God like a child will not enter it [at] [all]." And He took them in His arms and [began] blessing them, laying His hands on them.

MARK 10:13–16

∽

IT SEEMS THAT many moms and dads were taking their children to Jesus so that He could touch and bless them. It also seems that Jesus' disciples did not think the children should take up His valuable time. This may very well speak to their view of children as shaped by the prevailing culture of that day. Children in those days and times did not matter as much as adults, and thus were overlooked by society. The problem with this view is that it does not represent how God feels.

The kingdom of God had been offered to the whole world—children included. To see the disciples try to exclude the children brought an intense emotional response from Jesus. With the gift of eternal life offered to the whole world, a response was needed by each individual. The offer needed to be received by young and old. Jesus made it very clear that it must be received in childlike trust. He made it clear that only those who were able to trust Him like a child would see the Kingdom of God.

God's spiritual rule in our lives today is only possible when we trust Him. This means we must trust with wild abandon—just as children trust those they know and love. When a child jumps from a diving board into the arms of his father treading water in the deep end of a swimming pool, the child is showing trust. When a child sits down to a table full of food each night and does not demand to know how and when the parents secured the food, he is showing trust. When a child climbs into the back seat of a car and allows her mother to drive her to piano lessons each Thursday after school, she is showing trust.

When a man, woman, or child admits his sin to God and confesses he is helpless to help himself, he is showing trust. When a person communicates clearly his belief that Jesus' work on the cross and His resurrection are enough to cancel his own sin, he is showing trust. Jesus said, ". . . for the kingdom of God belongs to such as these."

In our quest to be "big boys and girls" and in our quest to be big strong adults, let's not forget the quality Christ calls for in regards to our involvement with Him and His kingdom. Childlike is not the same as childish. Childlike is honorable and necessary. Childish is ugly and useless. Childlike is the quality that allows us to see God for who He is and yet know we have free access to Him through His Son.

Don't let anyone or anything hinder you from approaching Jesus. Don't let your "big boy" pride or your "big girl" attitude get in the way. He is the Heavenly Father that provides for His children, and He desires for us to accept that willingly. Just as Jesus took those children in His arms to bless them that day, He desires to embrace you and me. I hope we never grow up enough to reject that fact of life. Childlike faith puts us in the arms of our loving heavenly Father. Let nothing hinder your approach to Him.

Security In Eternity

As He was setting out on a journey, a man ran up to Him and knelt before Him, and asked Him, "Good Teacher, what shall I do to inherit eternal life?" And Jesus said to him, "Why do you call Me good? No one is good except God alone. You know the commandments, 'DO NOT MURDER, DO NOT COMMIT ADULTERY, DO NOT STEAL, DO NOT BEAR FALSE WITNESS, Do not defraud, HONOR YOUR FATHER AND MOTHER.'" And he said to Him, "Teacher, I have kept all these things from my youth up." Looking at him, Jesus felt a love for him and said to him, "One thing you lack: go and sell all you possess and give to the poor, and you will have treasure in heaven; and come, follow Me." But at these words he was saddened, and he went away grieving, for he was one who owned much property.

MARK 10:17–22

THIS WEALTHY YOUNG man looked as if he had gotten it. He knelt before Jesus and called Him "good teacher." He believed in the afterlife and desired to secure his place in eternity. He apparently did not lack good morals since he was able to confidently assure Jesus that he had mastered all the commandments that pertained to human relationships.

Ever since he was twelve years old (the age of accountability in Jewish culture) he had never murdered another human, he had never had sex outside the marriage covenant, he never took something that wasn't his, he never said something about someone that wasn't true, and he had never dishonored his mom and dad. His human relationships were in tip-top shape. His question to Jesus was basically, *Does this give me security in eternity?*

The answer from Jesus was a definite "no," but in order to demonstrate and illustrate this man's spiritual dilemma, Jesus asked him to do something that would reveal the truth. Jesus desired for this man to know that eternal security had nothing to do with what one *does* or *doesn't do*, but rather in Whom one trusts. Eternal life is a gift that must be received, not a payment for services rendered. Our human relationships could be in tip-top shape, and yet, if the relationship with God is still broken, there can be no eternal security.

The question that had to be answered in this young man's heart was simply, *Will I trust God's Messiah for forgiveness or will I trust my own efforts at winning Him over?* The best way to reveal what this man had placed his trust in was to ask him to let go of it and embrace the Lord. The call to sell all his possessions and give the proceeds to the poor was a unique call to this man who trusted his money more than his Maker. He loved the gift more than the Giver. He was devoted to the security of gold rather than the security of God. We know this because he walked away from Jesus very sad "for he was one who owned much property."

Money may not be what separates you from God. It happened to be the stumbling block for this one individual, but the same may not be true for you. When Jesus asked this man to follow Him, He was indicating the path He was walking on His way to a Jerusalem cross. Jesus, out of love for this man, asked him to trust only in His work on the cross for his eternal security. He was asking him to put down his little god and embrace the one true big God.

What little god are you holding on to? Are you holding on to the little god called "good works"? Are you holding on to the little god known as "I'm not as bad as the next guy"? Are you trusting the little god known as "I go to church therefore I'm okay"? Works, comparison, and church activity do not repair the spiritual damage done by our rebellion. Just as money doesn't cure the spiritual disease known as "sin," neither does good works nor good intentions. Only Christ can cure the disease of sin.

According to Jesus, this man lacked only one thing—faith alone in Christ alone. Is that one thing lacking in your life today? If so, there is still no security in your eternity. Security comes only as we embrace the work of Christ on the cross and His resurrection from the dead. Only then will our relationship with God be counted as "tip-top."

Heaven's Currency

And Jesus, looking around, said to His disciples, "How
hard it will be for those who are wealthy to enter the
kingdom of God!" The disciples were amazed at His
words. But Jesus answered again and said to them,
"Children, how hard it is to enter the kingdom of God! It
is easier for a camel to go through the eye of a needle than
for a rich man to enter the kingdom of God." They were
even more astonished and said to Him, "Then who can
be saved?" Looking at them, Jesus said, "With people it is
impossible, but not with God; for all things are possible
with God."

MARK 10:23–27

RICH PEOPLE IN those days must have been accustomed to buying
their way into clubs, organizations, positions of leadership, as well
as positions of influence. That may be why the disciples were so
shocked to hear Jesus speak of how difficult it is for the rich to
enter the kingdom of God. Their shock is understandable as we
begin to recognize that wealth, in the Jewish culture of that day,
signified God's blessing and would be considered a help rather than
a hindrance when it came to gaining God's favor.

Jesus made it quite clear, however, that heaven uses a different
currency. When it comes to heaven, Jesus is basically saying to us
all, "Your money is no good here!" Jesus employed hyperbole once
again when He compared the impossibility of a camel walking
through the eye of a sewing needle to the rich man's ability to enter
the kingdom of God with his own effort. What is impossible with
man (salvation) is not, however, impossible with God. Jesus spoke
of the salvation of the rich as *difficult* but not *impossible*. Their rescue
from spiritual darkness and despair is impossible if they continue
to run from God's rescue efforts and trust in their own. Their res-

cue from the deadly consequences of sin is not impossible, we are told, if they will exchange their currency (good works) for God's currency (grace).

A person who trusts in his own efforts and abilities to enter the kingdom of God is actually running from God. To trust our currency of good works is to run from God's currency called grace. To trust in anything other than God's grace and work, which was provided by the death and resurrection of Jesus, is to run away from the Rescuer.

In 1981, a Minnesota radio station reported a story about a stolen car in California. Police were staging an intense search for the vehicle and the driver, even to the point of placing announcements on local radio stations to contact the thief. On the front seat of the stolen car sat a box of crackers that, unbeknownst to the thief, were laced with poison. The car owner had intended to use the crackers as rat bait. The police and the owner of the VW Bug were more interested in apprehending the thief to save his life than to recover the car. So often when we run from God, we feel it is to escape his punishment. But what we are actually doing is eluding his rescue.

If you are trusting in anything other than the completed work of Christ on the cross and His resurrection for your rescue, keep in mind the ridiculous picture of a camel trying to go through the eye of a sewing needle. That impossibility is to remind you and me of how futile our own efforts are. If you have friends or family members trusting in anything other than Christ, continue praying that they will stop running from the Rescuer. Communicate as clearly and graciously as you can that their efforts at "self rescue" are impossible. Tell them that their "money" is no good in heaven. Let them know that grace is heaven's currency. Also let them know that the exchange rate is really good right now.

Blessings and Beatings

Peter began to say to Him, "Behold, we have left
everything and followed You." Jesus said, "Truly I say to
you, there is no one who has left house or brothers or
sisters or mother or father or children or farms, for My
sake and for the gospel's sake, but that he will receive a
hundred times as much now in the present age, houses and
brothers and sisters and mothers and children and farms,
along with persecutions; and in the age to come, eternal
life. But many [who are] first will be last, and the last, first."

MARK 10:28–31

❧

JESUS MADE IT very clear that there was a tremendous cost to discipleship. The young man who sadly walked away from Jesus because
he owned much property was neither ready to receive the gift of
salvation nor willing to pay the price of discipleship. If only he had
stayed around long enough to hear the whole story, he may have
reconsidered.

Peter, speaking on behalf of the disciples, affirmed to Jesus that
they had left everything to follow Him. Jesus affirmed to the disciples that anyone who would leave family and farm would receive
both blessings and beatings. Jesus did not candy-coat the tremendous cost of discipleship. Most of us would say we are ready for the
blessings that come from discipleship, but I wonder if we are truly
ready for the beatings.

Let's first consider the blessings. Christ clearly stated that all who
leave their families and their farms for His sake and the sake of the
gospel would "receive a hundred times as much now in the present
age . . ." The "age" He was referring to is the time between His first
and second coming. Jesus was promising that all the physical family
members left behind in the quest to follow Him would be replaced
with spiritual family members who would bring blessings into their

lives. The promise was that no one follows Jesus alone. His disciples would be given loving and lasting spiritual family members as a result of their courage to leave behind physical family and farms.

Jesus also mentioned beatings or persecutions. Jesus was not saying that everyone's physical family would hate him for his faith. What Jesus was saying is that following Him would bring persecution from the world that hates Him. The disciples were told, in no uncertain terms, that the journey of discipleship would not be without bumps and bruises. The journey to the cross was about a journey to rejections, beatings, and a painful death. Those who walk with Jesus would be persecuted with Jesus. I have a feeling the rich young ruler sensed this very thing and walked away.

Are you wanting to walk away from Jesus, too? Does the sound of blessings draw you in, and yet the seriousness of beatings drives you away? Do you want the one and not the other? You must decide. Remember what is on the other side of death. Jesus summed it up for His friends in two words—eternal life. The gift of grace is free, but the blessings of discipleship cost us everything. Let's consider taking a walk with Jesus that goes all the way to the cross. Rejections and beatings that lead to a painful death ultimately lead us to the blessings of deep and eternal life. Let's not walk away from Jesus now. We must keep going even if it means we are misunderstood and hated by our families. To lose it all for the sake of Christ and the gospel simply makes room for receiving a hundred times as much in return.

If we must take a beating for being followers of Jesus in this present age, then so be it. But let's also remember what awaits us in the age to come: eternal life with brothers, sisters, mothers, fathers, and children. And if there is a farm or two thrown in on top of that, you will definitely not hear me complaining. I will be too busy counting my blessings!

Amazed And Fearful

They were on the road going up to Jerusalem, and Jesus
was walking on ahead of them; and they were amazed,
and those who followed were fearful. And again He took
the twelve aside and began to tell them what was going
to happen to Him, [saying], "Behold, we are going up to
Jerusalem, and the Son of Man will be delivered to the
chief priests and the scribes; and they will condemn Him
to death and will hand Him over to the Gentiles. They will
mock Him and spit on Him, and scourge Him and kill
[Him], and three days later He will rise again."

MARK 10:32–34

WE ARE TOLD that as Jesus led His disciples on the road to Jerusalem
they were walking in astonishment and fear. That mixture of emotions can lead to inner confusion and conflict. On the one hand, the
disciples were astonished or amazed at the determination Jesus had
as He progressed toward Jerusalem. He had told them twice about
what awaited Him, and yet He was leading the way. No wonder
fear was washing over them. They were following Him into some
very dark and dangerous days.

As if things were not bad enough, Jesus stopped the procession
and pulled everyone in close. His third prediction of what was waiting for Him was the most precise and detailed. Many things would
happen to Him and most of them were terrible. He described being
betrayed, condemned, mocked, spat on, and flogged. Someone was
going to turn Him in. Someone else was going to judge and condemn Him. A group of folks would make fun of Him as "a king,"
while His body would be showered with human spit. His back
would be thrashed with a whip laced with sharp stones, broken bits
of bone, and shards of glass. Jesus was walking into the darkest days
of His life, and He was being very honest with His friends about

what was going to happen. Who wouldn't be afraid?

I believe the brief rest stop they took on the side of the road would have been a complete bust if He had not completed the picture for them. Though He was straightforward and honest about the eventual outcome, I wonder if they really heard the words "and three days later He will rise again." If they did not listen closely, they missed the best part of the prediction. If they did not pay close attention, their hearts, minds, and souls would be stuck in the terrible darkness of the crucifixion and not able to move into the wonderful light of the resurrection. "Three days later" is just seventy-two hours, but can be the difference between life and death for some if they fail to understand the significance.

Our journeys with Jesus contain moments of both amazement and fear. We are continually astonished by His love for us even though we continually fail to love Him back. Our hearts are overwhelmed with amazement at His determination to see us move through the darkness of sin's terrible grip and into the wonderful light of resurrection living. We stand amazed at Jesus' dedication to His Father's glory.

But we are also afraid. I believe our flesh's fear of sacrifice is part of what keeps us from following Jesus with the same determination, love, and commitment with which He marched into Jerusalem. I also believe, however, that if we would embrace the words "and three days later He will rise again," we would realize we have been given the same determination, love, and commitment Jesus possesses. Let's continue our journeys with Jesus with our God-given determination, love, and commitment. Yes, Jesus leads His friends into some very dark and dangerous times, but He also leads them through those dark times into the light of resurrection. Let's stand amazed while we acknowledge our fear, but let's also keep walking with Jesus toward the cross. For what lies just seventy-two hours on the other side of that cross actually translates into an eternity full of amazement and void of all fear. Very much worth the journey, wouldn't you say?

The Cup of Christ

James and John, the two sons of Zebedee, came up to
Jesus, saying, "Teacher, we want You to do for us whatever
we ask of You." And He said to them, "What do you want
Me to do for you?" They said to Him, "Grant that we may
sit, one on Your right and one on [Your] left, in Your glory."
But Jesus said to them, "You do not know what you are
asking. Are you able to drink the cup that I drink, or to
be baptized with the baptism with which I am baptized?"
They said to Him, "We are able." And Jesus said to them,
"The cup that I drink you shall drink; and you shall be
baptized with the baptism with which I am baptized. But
to sit on My right or on [My] left, this is not Mine to give;
but it is for those for whom it has been prepared."

MARK 10:35–40

THE TWO SONS of Zebedee, James and John, made a huge request of
Jesus as they visited with Him about His coming kingdom. Their
request was to occupy the top two positions in His administra-
tion. Their personal vision for themselves had one of them on His
left and the other on His right. They were asking for honor in the
Kingdom of God. It is not clear whether or not they tried to have
this conversation in private, but we do find out later that when the
other ten disciples heard about the request, they were quite upset. It
seems that James and John were not the only ones desiring honor.

Jesus knew what they were asking for, but did *they* know what
they were asking for? They probably did not know that to ask for
a share in His honor was to ask for a share of His sufferings. The
topic of suffering continued to come up in regard to their status
as disciples because one does not share in the honor if one does
not share in the suffering. Strong disciples know the reality of both
worlds. Honor comes after the suffering. Jesus wanted them to be

very clear in their understanding of this fact, and so He asked them if they were able "to drink the cup" that He would drink or "to be baptized with the baptism" with which He would be baptized.

Jesus had a unique "cup" to drink and a unique "baptism" to experience. The Old Testament picture of a "cup" was either one of joy, as in "my cup overflows" as seen in Psalm 23:5, or one of judgment, as in "the cup of His anger" as seen in Isaiah 51:17. Jesus' cup was the cup of God's judgment upon sin. God's full righteous justice and fury were soon going to come down on Jesus as He hung on the cross outside of Jerusalem. This was a unique "cup" which was only for Him. His "baptism" had the same subject of judgment in mind since being underwater was an Old Testament picture of being besieged by catastrophe. Taking on the full burden of God's judgment for the world's sin involved the crushing weight of suffering culminating in His death. Again, a very unique "baptism" for Jesus. The disciples would not be able to drink that specific cup or experience that specific baptism because of Jesus' unique role as Savior. But there was still a way to experience His honor.

Jesus assured them that, in a certain sense, His "cup" and "baptism" would be theirs as well. Not only would they enjoy all the benefits of His sacrificial death on their behalf, but they would feel the pain of suffering as His disciples. As it turned out, James was the first disciple to be killed for his faith, while John was the last disciple to die after many years of persecution.

The request from these loving and devoted followers of Christ was turned down by Jesus. The highest physical places of honor were not His to assign. His Father would make those assignments in due time. What these two wonderful brothers did experience, however, was the honor of dying for their King. Their "cup" and "baptism" was a reflection of their Savior's suffering. Let's be sure that the "cup" from which we drink is a reflection of the "cup" of Christ. It is only then that we will know the joy of a cup that overflows! It is only then that we will know what it is to obtain honor in His kingdom.

The Descent To Greatness

Hearing [this], the ten began to feel indignant with James
and John. Calling them to Himself, Jesus said to them,
"You know that those who are recognized as rulers of the
Gentiles lord it over them; and their great men exercise
authority over them. But it is not this way among you, but
whoever wishes to become great among you shall be your
servant; and whoever wishes to be first among you shall
be slave of all. For even the Son of Man did not come to
be served, but to serve, and to give His life a ransom for
many."

MARK 10:41–45

THE OTHER TEN disciples were quite upset with James and John
for requesting the top two positions of honor in Christ's kingdom.
Their irritation must have been obvious to Jesus because He called
a time out for an important team meeting. If the issue of greatness was not settled right then and there, the rest of the journey to
Jerusalem could have been fraught with resentment and bitterness,
as well as a serious power struggle as each one of them tried to
ascend to greatness.

Jesus first addressed what they did know and then addressed
what they did not know. What they did know was that the Gentile
(nice way of saying pagan) leaders were brutal in their leadership.
To them, greatness was measured by the intensity of their brutality.
To lord over someone was to stand over that person with brute
force demanding submissiveness. Jesus said the disciples knew this.
I would imagine He wanted them to think long and hard about
whether that is really how they wanted to be known. Jesus cast a
whole different vision for them by saying, "But it is not this way
among you . . . ."

Jesus then told them something they did not know. Jesus described a wonderful contrast to the pagan's ascent to greatness that was marked by selfishness and brutishness. Jesus' vision for His friends mapped out a wonderful path toward true greatness sanctioned by God Himself. Notice that He neither chastised them for wishing to be great nor scolded them for desiring to be first. He actually mapped out the journey to greatness for them. Jesus mapped out the *descent to greatness.*

I can only imagine the look on their faces as He described the journey *down* to greatness, rather than the clawing and grabbing they were used to as people climbed their way to "the top" (wherever that is). The journey He described to those He passionately loved was a journey of a servant and a slave. He shared His vision for them to step out of the limelight and into the shadow of the other. He walked them down the humble path of a slave who did not sit at the table, but rather set the table. His vision for their life involved their being at the end of the line, rather than the head of the line. He wanted them to be just like Him.

The great Jesus of Nazareth, whose favorite title for Himself was "Son of Man" rather than "Son of God," came right out and said that He came "not to be served, but to serve." Jesus took the descent to greatness one step further when He described His mission as a giving up of His life as a ransom for many. The Savior was really a servant. The Living Word spoke of dying. The King was actually a slave. Jesus pulled the team together to announce that the greatest one on the team is really the water boy.

Let's put ourselves in the huddle as we hear the challenge to descend to greatness. Let's make a conscience decision to walk in another's shadow as we serve them with humility. Let's serve our friends, family, and bosses with the joy of the Lord rather than the jealousy of the flesh. A world of servants is a world with very little clawing and grabbing. It is a world with very little indignation. It is a world with people willingly and joyfully descending to the greatness mapped out for them by their Creator. It is a world where the unknown water boy delivers a cool cup of water to the well-known quarterback and though the stadium does not erupt in wild and frenzied cheers, his greatness is recorded and his reward is reserved. A world of servants is a great world!

Messiah's Mercy

Then they came to Jericho. And as He was leaving Jericho
with His disciples and a large crowd, a blind beggar
[named] Bartimaeus, the son of Timaeus, was sitting by
the road. When he heard that it was Jesus the Nazarene,
he began to cry out and say, "Jesus, Son of David, have
mercy on me!" Many were sternly telling him to be quiet,
but he kept crying out all the more, "Son of David, have
mercy on me!" And Jesus stopped and said, "Call him
[here]." So they called the blind man, saying to him, "Take
courage, stand up! He is calling for you." Throwing aside
his cloak, he jumped up and came to Jesus. And answering
him, Jesus said, "What do you want Me to do for you?"
And the blind man said to Him, "Rabboni, [I want] to
regain my sight!" And Jesus said to him, "Go; your faith
has made you well." Immediately he regained his sight and
[began] following Him on the road.

MARK 10:46–52

THE NEW TESTAMENT Jericho was built not far from the Old
Testament Jericho and was apparently a very wealthy town. It was
built by Herod the Great and served as his winter retreat. Because
of the city's great wealth, it was not uncommon to see many unnamed beggars with their outer cloaks spread before them to collect money from those who would take pity on them. This passage
introduces us to a beggar whose name we *do* know. We meet blind
Bartimaeus, the son of Timaeus, as he sits along the road dependent on the alms of those who would notice. While he would take
the money of the masses, what he really needed was the mercy of
the Messiah.

Jerusalem was less than twenty miles away from Jericho and
Passover was just days away. A large crowd of Passover pilgrims

was walking along this road at the same time Jesus and His disciples were. The crowd was abuzz about Jesus and the fact that many were calling Him Israel's Messiah. There is a very good chance arguments broke out regarding the true identity of Jesus—arguments that were overheard by a blind man in tremendous need of a Savior. Upon hearing it was Jesus, Bartimaeus cried out to Jesus calling Him "Son of David." This title gave away the fact that Bartimaeus had heard of the wonderful things Jesus had been doing and that he believed Him to be the Messiah who was to come through the blood line of King David. Many people attempted to silence Bartimaeus as he proclaimed his faith in Jesus as Messiah.

Those who were attempting to silence him could have been "unbelievers" who were offended by Bartimaeus' proclamation. However, those who were attempting to silence him could have been the disciples. The disciples may have been trying to protect Jesus' valuable time as He made His determined march toward Jerusalem. The fact that Jesus stopped and called Bartimaeus to Himself shows His acceptance of the title (touché unbelievers) as well as His willingness to take time for those in need (touché disciples).

Jesus knew what Bartimaeus needed. He wasn't gathering information. He asked the question "What do you want Me to do for you?" so that Bartimaeus could articulate, in his own words, the great need in his life. It gave him a chance to admit his inability to save himself. The word *rabboni* looks and sounds a lot like the word *rabbi*, which means "teacher." "Rabboni" has a much larger position in mind, meaning, "My Master and my Lord." Bartimaeus was asking for the Messiah's mercy, not the teacher's training. Bartimaeus had the Anointed One's attention and was now asking for His mercy.

Every day affords us repeated opportunities to express our own inabilities and miseries to God. Whether we want to admit it or not, those inabilities and miseries have put us on Beggar's Row. We beg for attention in a busy and fast-paced world. We beg for significance in a world that is addicted to fame. We beg for love in a world that defaults to lust. We beg for clarity in a world of confusing alternatives. Let's stop begging of people and start crying to God. Let's cry for Messiah's mercy. If the crowd tries to stop us, we must cry that much louder. He is calling us to Himself this very day. We have *His* attention so it is now time to express *our* need. He is the Messiah who is not too busy to stop for us. Bartimaeus received his sight that day and began to follow Jesus. Let's get in line with him. Messiah's mercy is calling us to that journey.

Looks Can Be Deceiving

As they approached Jerusalem, at Bethphage and Bethany, near the Mount of Olives, He sent two of His disciples, and said to them, "Go into the village opposite you, and immediately as you enter it, you will find a colt tied [there], on which no one yet has ever sat; untie it and bring it [here]. If anyone says to you, 'Why are you doing this?' you say, 'The Lord has need of it'; and immediately he will send it back here." They went away and found a colt tied at the door, outside in the street; and they untied it. Some of the bystanders were saying to them, "What are you doing, untying the colt?" They spoke to them just as Jesus had told [them], and they gave them permission. They brought the colt to Jesus and put their coats on it; and He sat on it. And many spread their coats in the road, and others [spread] leafy branches which they had cut from the fields. Those who went in front and those who followed were shouting: "Hosanna! BLESSED IS HE WHO COMES IN THE NAME OF THE LORD; Blessed [is] the coming kingdom of our father David; Hosanna in the highest!"

Jesus entered Jerusalem [and came] into the temple; and after looking around at everything, He left for Bethany with the twelve, since it was already late.

MARK 11:1–11

✥

I WOULD IMAGINE Jesus did not enter Jerusalem the way other kings would have. The way I picture it, other kings would enter the city with military bands playing patriotic tunes, thousands of prearranged admirers lining the street, and ticker tape falling from the rooftops. I imagine other kings would ride a white stallion down a beautiful clean road, surrounded by his armies, and wearing his royal attire. No, Jesus did not enter the city as other kings would have. He entered the city looking more like a ruffian than a ruler.

Consider that He rode a borrowed colt. He wore regular, rather than regal, clothes, and sat on a makeshift saddle. In lieu of floating ticker tape, Jesus was greeted with leafy sticks and used clothing laid before Him as a covering for the dusty road He traveled. The crowd could probably be counted in the hundreds rather than thousands. In the absence of a marching band, the crowd chanted portions of Psalms. These Psalms revealed the people's hope that Jesus would soon stop *pretending* to be king and actually call them to arms and lead them to a violent overthrow of the occupying Roman forces. Many in the crowd believed Him to be the conquering Messiah but they could not help but have their doubts. He certainly did not look like a conquering Messiah.

What did He look like? A grown man riding a small donkey surely did not overwhelm or impress throngs of people. Those who led the way were calling out "Hosanna" which basically means, "Save us now!" The invasion seemed to be getting off to a really slow start. We must remember, however, looks can be deceiving.

Let's look at the passage carefully for subtle signs of Jesus' identity as the triumphant King. His sending two of His friends into town to secure the colt from a specific location and predicting the conversation is not the work of a mere mortal. His ability to ride an unbroken colt shows the power of the Creator over His creation. Identifying Himself as "the Lord" is a bold proclamation of deity that can't be ignored. Patiently surveying the activity at the temple and then personally picking the proper time to make changes is the work of a meek (which actually means power under control) and mild Messiah. The King entered the world as a small and vulnerable baby thirty-three years earlier and only a few shepherds showed up to say, "Wow!" The King later entered Jerusalem right in front of their eyes and only a small crowd said, "Welcome." Too many were deceived by appearances.

Are you and I being deceived by appearances even today? Has the Jesus we have been expecting been a "no show" for us? Have we been looking for the conquering Messiah and been tremendously disappointed in the One who has arrived? It happens to us all. We desperately long for Him to enter our lives on a powerful white stallion swinging a sword of justice, and yet miss the fact that He has entered on His humble colt offering grace for sin. Are we ready to line the dusty roads of our hearts with whatever "leafy branches" we can find in hopes He will pick them up and do something wonderful with them? Are we calling out for Him to mend our wounded lives, heal our struggling marriages, encourage our discouraged kids, renew our lagging spirits, or even take us in His arms and tell us it is all going to be okay? I wonder what would happen if we stopped looking for a certain kind of Messiah and simply embraced the One who has revealed Himself in humility and meekness. What would happen if we simply embraced the suffering Messiah who came to die so that we would thrive? What if we simply trusted Him in the midst of the wounds, struggles, discouragements, laggings, and longings? I would imagine it would look a lot like a King who has come home to heal and come home to rule!

All Show?

On the next day, when they had left Bethany, He became
hungry. Seeing at a distance a fig tree in leaf, He went [to
see] if perhaps He would find anything on it; and when
He came to it, He found nothing but leaves, for it was not
the season for figs. He said to it, "May no one ever eat fruit
from you again!" And His disciples were listening. . . .

As they were passing by in the morning, they saw the
fig tree withered from the roots [up]. Being reminded,
Peter said to Him, "Rabbi, look, the fig tree which You
cursed has withered."

MARK 11:12–14 AND 20–21

IT SEEMS STRANGE that Jesus would be so harsh toward a tree that
did not have figs, knowing that "it was not the season for figs." What
was Jesus expecting? Was He expecting too much? What was going
on with the fig tree, and what is the lesson for you and me?

It may help to know that the encounter between Jesus and this
lone fig tree took place in mid-April. We know this because it was
the season of Passover, which took place annually at that time of
year. In the month of March, Palestinian fig trees produced edible
buds and then large green leaves. The buds were food for the poor.
It was free food for the picking. Those buds that went uneaten
would eventually fall to the ground as figs appeared in late April or
early May. It made sense for Jesus to see the large green leaves and
expect to find buds to eat. The lack of buds was a strong indication
that the tree would not produce any figs that year. The tree had the
"look" of a productive tree, but it did not have the "life" of a productive tree. It was all show.

The fact that these verses sandwich the encounter Jesus had
with the "money changers" in the temple indicates that Christ was
forecasting His approaching judgment on the nation of Israel. Her

"look" of life could be seen in the busyness of religious activity and yet did not produce the "fruit" of a productive spiritual journey of faith. The people of Israel were all show and no go when it came to spiritual life. They were like the fig tree.

How are you doing in this area of your life? Is there a lot of religious activity that gives the "look" of spiritual life and yet the "fruit" that's expected is lacking? The Scripture identifies this fruit as "love, joy, peace, patience, kindness, goodness, faithfulness, gentleness, self-control . . . ." (Galatians 5:22 and 23). This fruit is natural to a spiritual person who is filled and controlled by the Spirit of God. It is natural for the spiritual man or woman to blossom with this fruit because of the life-giving power of the Holy Spirit. Religious activity does not produce spiritual fruit. Reading the Bible apart from the illuminating power of the Holy Spirit is merely religious activity. Attending church in order to relieve guilt has the "look" of a follower of Christ but lacks the life. Doing good for the poor in order to feel better about our wealth is just a really pretty "leaf" on our tree, but the lack of fruit—spiritual fruit—rats us out. We can definitely have the "look" and not the "life."

Israel's lack of productive spiritual life resulted from her rejection of Jesus as Messiah. A person's acceptance of Him as Messiah brings new life from the inside out. Life becomes more about *who* we are in Christ because of His work in us than it does about *what* we do for Christ as merely religious workers. The life that comes from within produces fruit that is nourishing and refreshing to the world around us. It produces a life that is pleasing to the Gardener.

Jesus is calling us to a deep spiritual life with Him that produces nourishing fruit. The tree had the "look" but did not have the "life." Let's commit ourselves to Him in such a way that what was true about the fig tree would not be true about us. Let's not be all show and no go. A productive spiritual life comes from being *with* Jesus not being busy *for* Jesus. There is a difference.

Sin Is Ripping Us Off

Then they came to Jerusalem. And He entered the temple and began to drive out those who were buying and selling in the temple, and overturned the tables of the money changers and the seats of those who were selling doves; and He would not permit anyone to carry merchandise through the temple. And He [began] to teach and say to them, "Is it not written, 'MY HOUSE SHALL BE CALLED A HOUSE OF PRAYER FOR ALL THE NATIONS'? But you have made it a ROBBERS' DEN." The chief priests and the scribes heard [this], and [began] seeking how to destroy Him; for they were afraid of Him, for the whole crowd was astonished at His teaching.

When evening came, they would go out of the city.

MARK 11:15–19

⌘

THE OUTER COURT of the temple area was set apart for use by the Gentiles. Though they were not allowed to go beyond the outer court, they were allowed to worship God by participating in the annual sacrifices that recalled the wonderful way God redeemed Israel out of Egypt. The redeeming grace of God was (and is) for all nations, so a place in the temple area was set aside for the Gentiles. Unfortunately, that area had become one big rip-off and that angered Jesus.

When Christ entered the temple area and saw the rip-off that was happening by way of money changing and selling of "ritually pure" items needed for the upcoming sacrifices, he became very *angry* and very *active*. Three types of currency were in use in those days. There was Roman currency (imperial), Greek currency (provincial), and Jewish currency (local). The Greek and Roman currency had human images on them which put them in the "idolatrous" category and could not be used to pay the temple tax. Caiaphas, the high priest, allowed this innovative market to be set up as a convenience for "out-of-towners" who traveled long distances without a sacrificial animal and needed to buy one on site. They could also exchange their imperial and provincial money for the required Tyrian coinage. This system obviously allowed for corruption, extortion, and fraud. The system became a rip-off.

Think about the scandal of God's special place, designed for His people to connect with Him through worship and prayer, being turned into a robber's cave. His holy place was now a hideout for those who would take advantage of the poor and vulnerable. Who was to say whether your sacrificial animal was pure or not? You could be told your animal was not fit for sacrifice (not knowing any better) and be forced to buy one that was. It would not be uncommon to see your "trade-in" sold later to another unsuspecting traveler. Jesus did not want to see this happen in His house of prayer. Jesus took action in His anger.

What sin is ripping you off today? What sin is robbing you of the joy and the life God designed for you? Too often what we think profits us is really robbing us. We use dishonesty to protect us rather than depending on God for that needed protection. The sin of greed keeps us working more for what we want than what we need. Lust buries us in the make-believe world of significance and sentiment and thus squelches true love. Our enemy has set up shop in our neighborhood and is convincing us to make unholy "exchanges." He is convincing us to exchange conscientiousness for perfectionism, communication for gossip, self-care for selfishness, enjoyment of life for intemperance, anger for rage, physical appetite for gluttony, ability to profit for greed, and physical rest for laziness. Sin rips us off and it is not making us angry. Jesus showed great strength, courage, emotion, presence, and passion by taking on the crowd in the temple. His love for the "little guy" moved Him to take on the powers that be. His authority was demonstrated by His words (He taught them) and His works (He turned over their tables).

Let's allow Jesus to enter our hearts today to clean house. Let's invite Him in to rid us of the sin that is ripping us off. Though it startles us, His anger and His action are actually good for our lives. If we listen, He will *teach* us. If we obey, He will *transform* us. Either way, we will profit because we will no longer let sin rip us off!

Asking For The Impossible

And Jesus answered saying to them, "Have faith in God.
Truly I say to you, whoever says to this mountain, 'Be
taken up and cast into the sea,' and does not doubt in his
heart, but believes that what he says is going to happen,
it will be [granted] him. Therefore I say to you, all things
for which you pray and ask, believe that you have received
them, and they will be [granted] you."

MARK 11:22–24

IN THE CONTEXT of hearing and seeing Jesus' power to curse the
tree and cleanse the temple, Christ urged His friends to have faith
in God. A good definition of faith might be to put one's full confidence in the full power and goodness of God. Christ was calling
His friends to believe and trust in the never-ending strength and
decency of God. It is what He is calling you and me to do as well.

Utilizing hyperbole once again, Jesus taught about the power
of faith to accomplish great things. To call on the Mount of Olives
(or any other immovable barrier) to be uprooted and moved into
the sea by faith is to call on God's power to make the impossible
happen.

Jesus puts a huge condition on the privilege of experiencing this
kind of answered prayer. The condition is that *doubt* must lose out
to *belief*. For the disciples to demonstrate such unwavering faith
in God, they would be living in blatant contrast to how Israel was
living. The nation of Israel, under the leadership of her religious
leaders, was doubting God's chosen Messiah, Jesus Christ. The ex-
hortation Jesus was giving His disciples was to "have faith in God."

There are so many immovable "mountains" in our lives, aren't
there? It is humanly impossible to save some marriages, turn children back to the Lord, restore hope to the hopeless, love to the
loveless, courage to the fearful, and joy to the sorrowful. But noth-

ing is impossible to the all-powerful and all-benevolent God of the universe. All is possible for Him. Human prayer moves the hand of God to do what no human can. Christ wanted His friends to believe this in such a way that they considered their request to be a "done deal." They were asked to live as if it were a *present tense* reality though the answer was a *future tense* certainty. Christ had already made it very clear in His teaching that all human prayer must be in accord with God's will. The answer God gives is then received by the faith that offered the request. This assures harmony between the Giver of all good things given and the receiver of all good things needed.

Jesus made it very clear that obedient believers receive God's generous and powerful response. It is obedient believers who know by experience that no circumstance or obstacle is impossible for God.

What are you facing today that you can now admit is impossible for you but not for God? It may be an issue of health, finance, relationships, spiritual vitality, or emotional lethargy. Any issue that touches your life can be that which is impossible for you, yet possible for God. Believing in the goodness and power of God draws us closer to His goodness and power. Resting in His goodness and power allows Him to be God and us to be human. Even better, it is faith that brings the two together.

Jesus Himself said that our faith can move mountains. How will we ever experience the sheer power and goodness of God if we stop asking Him for the impossible? You're right, we won't!

Forgive To Be Forgiven

"Whenever you stand praying, forgive, if you have
anything against anyone, so that your Father who is in
heaven will also forgive you your transgressions. [But
if you do not forgive, neither will your Father who is in
heaven forgive your transgressions.]"

MARK 11:25–26

JESUS WAS FINISHING some important teaching on prayer when, all
of a sudden, He connected forgiveness between you and me with
forgiveness between God and me. And I was just starting to like
what I was reading. Why did He have to make things so hard? I
find asking for forgiveness to be really easy while I find offering forgiveness to be very difficult. I am being honest about this because it
is a subject that cannot be ignored by either you or me.

I am sure I am not alone in this. Forgiveness is one of the easiest
things to ask for from God, and yet can be one of the most difficult things to offer a fellow human being struggling through life
. . . just like you and me. I am not sure I have gone through a single
day when I was not painfully aware of my need for someone in my
life to forgive me. I have offended a lot of people. I have said some
things that were insensitive and insincere. I have done some things
that have been selfish and brutish. I have pushed in line and crossed
the line. I have ignored the needs of others as I have hoarded toys
and treasure. I have been *very* human.

I, like you, have stood on the shores of God's ocean of forgiveness and received buckets of grace. I, like you, have not only received
and enjoyed God's *eternal* forgiveness, but also have benefited from
His *daily* forgiveness. It is His daily forgiveness that allows us to
walk with Him in true spiritual intimacy. We are allowed to stand
on the shores of His ocean of forgiveness and *drink* liberally of His
refreshing and rejuvenating grace; at the same time, we are called to

distribute forgiveness and grace to those who have offended us. Jesus did not make it easy when He said, "if you have *anything* against *anyone*" (emphasis added). He does not leave any wiggle room, does He? All offenses and all people are in view here. We cannot escape the scope or the seriousness of His words. He means business! If we refuse to *distribute* His grace on a daily basis, He refuses to *contribute* it on a daily basis. While we will never be cut off from His eternal forgiveness, the daily grace needed for intimacy is definitely refused.

I don't know about you, but I do not want to face life with that kind of separation between God and me. I need His daily forgiveness in order to live my life to the fullness He designed for me. To illustrate how important forgiveness is to our daily lives, consider what Karl Menniger, the famed psychiatrist, said. He once told a group of people that if he could convince the patients in psychiatric hospitals that their sins were forgiven, seventy-five percent of them could walk out the next day! Our offenses weigh us down. To have them lifted from us (forgiven) by God, we must lift them from (forgive) those around us.

Who do you need to forgive today? Who needs just a teaspoon of grace? Let's not think we can continue to dip into the great ocean of God's grace without being called to distribute it to that person who wounded us either yesterday or yesteryear. It does not work that way. Forgiveness is not just an eternal issue. It is a daily issue that needs daily attention. We must forgive to be forgiven.

Questioning God

They came again to Jerusalem. And as He was walking
in the temple, the chief priests and the scribes and the
elders came to Him, and [began] saying to Him, "By what
authority are You doing these things, or who gave You this
authority to do these things?" And Jesus said to them, "I
will ask you one question, and you answer Me, and [then]
I will tell you by what authority I do these things. Was
the baptism of John from heaven, or from men? Answer
Me." They [began] reasoning among themselves, saying, "If
we say, 'From heaven,' He will say, 'Then why did you not
believe him?' "But shall we say, 'From men'?"—they were
afraid of the people, for everyone considered John to have
been a real prophet. Answering Jesus, they said, "We do
not know." And Jesus said to them, "Nor will I tell you by
what authority I do these things."

MARK 11:27–33

⤬

THE RELIGIOUS LEADERS challenged Jesus by questioning His authority to "do these things." "These things" included His teaching
and His healing, but spoke specifically to His earlier incident of
clearing the temple of the sellers and money changers. The leadership was not happy to see what Jesus was doing and wanted to
know if He could authenticate His authority. Jesus was willing to
oblige ... with one condition. He would answer them *after* they
answered Him.

The chief priests, scribes, and elders were easily stumped by
Christ's question regarding John's baptism (from heaven or from
earth?) due to their fear of people and their unbelief in Jesus. In
playing out the conversation in their heads and their unholy huddle, they realized they were trapped. The ultimate conviction being,
"Then why did you not believe him?"

There are two things we must all watch for in our response to Jesus. First of all, we must not question God from unbelief. The second thing to watch for is setting aside belief because of fear. Faith leads to open and honest communication with God. He loves for His children to ask Him questions from their childlike faith. Discovering doctrine comes from our questions, and the end result is supposed to be discipline. The question that came from the priests, scribes, and elders was not about *discovery*, but rather *disrespect*. Keep in mind that disrespecting God gets the silence of God. "Nor will I tell you by what authority I do these things" was Jesus' way of announcing the silence of God brought on by their disrespectful unbelief.

Dynamic discovery is an exciting part of the believer's journey of faith. Jesus longs for us to "seek" and to "ask." Jesus promised we would "find" and "receive" when we asked in faith. This discovery comes from a childlike faith that trusts in the Heavenly Father to accept our honest doubts and confusion in the midst of our growing and maturing faith. This is not what Jesus was responding to in His encounter with the priests, scribes, and elders. He was responding to their disrespectful challenge brought on by unbelief. Their group discussion in hushed tones smoked them out as cowards. To admit that John's baptism was from heaven would show their lack of faith in his mission and ministry. To say his baptism was from man would put them at odds with the people they sought to control.

Being fearful of people and disrespectful of God brings our spiritual progress to a near standstill. Let's approach Jesus with a childlike faith that asks for a true understanding that comes from dynamic discovery. He is God the Son and He is to be respected and revered as such.

Jesus longs to hear our questions and is eager to aid us in our discovery of truth. It seems clear that the next step for us all would be to approach Jesus with the reverence He deserves and the childlike faith He demands. The silence of God is deafening when it comes by way of our disrespect. Go ahead, question God; but question Him out of respect and a sincere faith. He loves that!

We Can't Have It All

And He began to speak to them in parables: "A man PLANTED A VINEYARD AND PUT A WALL AROUND IT, AND DUG A VAT UNDER THE WINE PRESS AND BUILT A TOWER, and rented it out to vine-growers and went on a journey. At the [harvest] time he sent a slave to the vine-growers, in order to receive [some] of the produce of the vineyard from the vine-growers. They took him, and beat him and sent him away empty-handed. Again he sent them another slave, and they wounded him in the head, and treated him shamefully. And he sent another, and that one they killed; and [so with] many others, beating some and killing others. He had one more [to send], a beloved son; he sent him last [of all] to them, saying, 'They will respect my son.' But those vine-growers said to one another, 'This is the heir; come, let us kill him, and the inheritance will be ours!' They took him, and killed him and threw him out of the vineyard. What will the owner of the vineyard do? He will come and destroy the vine-growers, and will give the vineyard to others. Have you not even read this Scripture: 'THE STONE WHICH THE BUILDERS REJECTED, THIS BECAME THE CHIEF CORNER [stone]; THIS CAME ABOUT FROM THE LORD, AND IT IS MARVELOUS IN OUR EYES'?"

And they were seeking to seize Him, and [yet] they feared the people, for they understood that He spoke the parable against them. And [so] they left Him and went away.

MARK 12:1–12

❦

PARABOLIC TEACHING HAD two goals. One goal was to teach important truth to believers, and the other was to protect important truth from unbelievers. Jesus wanted to provide truth to His friends while protecting the truth from the unbelieving Pharisees. To do this, He "gift-wrapped" the truth in parables. The truth is there for the taking, it just has to be received and unwrapped with faith. The truth is *provided*, and yet is still *protected*.

In this parable, Jesus tells of three slaves being sent to the those tending the vineyard and those same three slaves being rejected. One was beaten, one was beaten badly, and one was beaten to death. The vine-growers were renting the vineyard and were to give a portion of the proceeds to the owner's representative. The vine-growers were treating the owner's representatives worse and worse because they "wanted it all."

The owner of the vineyard did not give up after three attempts to retrieve what was rightfully his. He persevered by sending more and more slaves. All were either beaten or killed. The last person sent was his own beloved son. *Surely they will respect my son!*

The vine-growers saw an opportunity in the last visit that was not in the previous visits. They saw a chance to *own* the vineyard. It would all be theirs if they killed the son. They may have assumed the owner was dead since it was the son coming to them. The law made provision for "squatters' rights" if no owner could be found. In their thinking, the inheritance would fall to them. Believing that lie, they killed the son and dumped the body.

Jesus asked a rhetorical question in order to make a very clear point about how the owner should respond. The owner's response was to destroy the workers and distribute the vineyard to others. Jesus' quoting of Psalm 118 (a Messianic psalm) indicated that He was the beloved Son who was going to be killed, and thus become the cornerstone on which the new builders (Gentiles) would build. The Pharisees' anger at Jesus was moving them to seize Him, but their fear of the people motivated them to simply walk away.

That which happened on a large national scale, in terms of turning away the "owner" in order to have it all, could very well take place on a smaller personal scale.

We must consider whether our quest to "have it all" has somehow caused us to turn God away from that which is rightfully His (our whole lives). It could help us if we keep in mind the strength and accuracy of the "cornerstone" on which we are building our lives. Christ has been set in place as the chief cornerstone of the Church and stands well-qualified to be the chief cornerstone of our lives. The Lord is worthy of our embrace of Him with open arms rather than our rejection of Him with closed fists. He deserves full access to our lives.

Christ is the owner and must be respected as such. Jesus made it quite clear that anyone who tries to "have it all" in his own effort is in danger of forfeiting that with which he has been entrusted. What is your response to the beloved Son?

A Life Rendered Well

Then they sent some of the Pharisees and Herodians to Him in order to trap Him in a statement. They came and said to Him, "Teacher, we know that You are truthful and defer to no one; for You are not partial to any, but teach the way of God in truth. Is it lawful to pay a poll-tax to Caesar, or not? Shall we pay or shall we not pay?" But He, knowing their hypocrisy, said to them, "Why are you testing Me? Bring Me a denarius to look at." They brought [one]. And He said to them, "Whose likeness and inscription is this?" And they said to Him, "Caesar's." And Jesus said to them, "Render to Caesar the things that are Caesar's, and to God the things that are God's." And they were amazed at Him.

MARK 12:13–17

⊗

JESUS KNEW THE hypocrisy of those trying to trap Him and He knew the trap they were so cleverly trying to set for Him. They *said* they knew Him to be truthful and impartial, but in reality, they did not believe that at all. Because they did not believe Jesus to be who He said He was, His words remained scrutinized for error and indictment. They may have thought flattery would cause Him to lower His defenses and thus allow them "to trap Him in a statement," but it did not work.

What a shame! If they had listened and submitted to Jesus' answer about taxes (a great question, I might add!) they would have gained tremendous insight into God's design for how believers are to live in the "real world" that contains those ever present certainties: death and taxes.

Jesus did not just give a cute and clever answer to avoid the trap. He gave the correct answer regarding a believer's responsibility in the area of taxes. The short and sweet answer is, *Pay what you owe!*

Those of us in the United States are fortunate because we are allowed to pay as *little* tax as possible as long as we correctly and lawfully utilize the system. While we are not required to pay more than we owe, we are required to pay *all* that we owe. We are able to take every credit and deduction that is legally ours as we "render to Caesar the things that are Caesar's." Jesus affirmed for us that paying the taxes we owe is our responsibility.

Jesus also spoke of another rendering. He spoke of rendering to God what is God's. We in the United States (and all over the world, really) have no "credits" or "deductions" to apply to this call to render. He is calling us to render our whole lives. This rendering goes beyond tithes and offerings. Our whole lives belong to Him.

What does it look like to render our lives to God? It includes, but is not limited to, our families and finances; our friends as well as our faith community; our feelings and our failures; our fun and our fears. There is no itemized deduction worksheet that allows us to keep back part of our lives. God is calling us to a full and complete rendering of our lives. There is no EZ form when it comes to following Jesus. It is straightforward and clear what He is calling us to, but there is nothing EZ about it.

If we want to think in terms of "credits and deductions" then we must embrace the credit awarded us by faith in Christ's work on the cross and His resurrection. The only deduction that we need to be concerned with is the deduction of guilt won for and awarded to us by Jesus Himself.

The reality of life is that some of our money is to go to "Caesar" (the IRS) while our whole lives are to go to God. If only the Pharisees, Sadducees, and Scribes had listened to Jesus, they would have gotten in on a great deal regarding eternal life and never once been forced to fill out a complicated form or schedule. They would have received a believer's "refund" (eternal life with Jesus) upon their death. A "refund" that beats, I might add, anything the IRS would ever send our way! Let's make it our goal to live a life rendered well.

The Difference Between Hope and Despair

[Some] Sadducees (who say that there is no resurrection) came to Jesus, and [began] questioning Him, saying, "Teacher, Moses wrote for us that IF A MAN'S BROTHER DIES and leaves behind a wife AND LEAVES NO CHILD, HIS BROTHER SHOULD MARRY THE WIFE AND RAISE UP CHILDREN TO HIS BROTHER. There were seven brothers; and the first took a wife, and died leaving no children. The second one married her, and died leaving behind no children; and the third likewise; and [so] all seven left no children. Last of all the woman died also. In the resurrection, when they rise again, which one's wife will she be? For all seven had married her." Jesus said to them, "Is this not the reason you are mistaken, that you do not understand the Scriptures or the power of God? For when they rise from the dead, they neither marry nor are given in marriage, but are like angels in heaven. But regarding the fact that the dead rise again, have you not read in the book of Moses, in the [passage] about [the burning] bush, how God spoke to him, saying, 'I AM THE GOD OF ABRAHAM, AND THE GOD OF ISAAC, and the God of Jacob'? He is not the God of the dead, but of the living; you are greatly mistaken."

MARK 12:18–27

❧

DURING THE TIME I wrote this book I officiated and attended several funerals. There were definitely mixed emotions for me as I felt both a deep sadness over the loss (from my perspective) and the joy of knowing that the person we were eulogizing was with Jesus.

I purposely took time to look into the faces of those around me, and I can tell you that I saw the look of *despair* in many of those in attendance. I also, however, witnessed a genuine look of *hope* in the faces of others. What made the difference?

Read Mark 12:18–27 and you will encounter the Sadducees. Those religious officials, a group of conservative priests who represented the aristocracy of the day, laid out a long and complicated "what if" for Jesus to see if His teaching on the resurrection would stand up. The scenario they laid out was simply a joyless smoke screen, and Jesus called them on it. He said, "... you are greatly mistaken."

The Sadducees did not believe in the resurrection from the dead (that's why they were sad-you-see). Their conservative mentality, along with their desire to see things remain as they were, led them to compromise politically with the occupying Roman force. This unholy alliance diminished their moral authority with the people, and they felt very threatened by the growing popularity of Jesus. The plan was to find a theological topic that would trip Him up.

Jesus let them know that their lack of understanding regarding life (here and beyond) was tied to their failure to understand the Scriptures or the power of God. The *Word* of God and the *work* of God in our lives are what bring us understanding and progress in the spiritual life. Allowing both to penetrate our living souls allows us to know the God of the living.

God affirmed to Moses that He was the God of Abraham, Isaac, and Jacob. These three men had "passed away," but were living. The Word of God, had the Sadducees embraced it, would have flooded their minds and souls with truth and understanding. It is too bad they were set in their ways and unable to receive the truth.

The great hope for us, in a day and age when death is all around us, is that we can know the God of the living. Death has no *final* bite for a believer. Death has no *ultimate* sting for those in Christ. The grave is not a dead end as some believe. Jesus affirmed to us that, "... he who believes in Me will live even if he dies" (John 11:25). To know the God of the living is to know the hope of what awaits. A life that is full and eternal comes only from God. This life is offered to you and me.

Let's allow the *Word* of God to give us understanding of life here and beyond. Let's rest in the *Power* of God take us into the eternal life He has promised. Because the Sadducees failed to trust both God's *Word* and *work,* they missed the blessings and hope of the resurrection life.

No long and complicated story about seven brothers marrying the same woman could stump the Lord. He is the God of the living and no complex story of death can confuse the issue of the eternal life He offers. Let's not only enjoy the life we have been given here, but let's also rejoice with great joy as we anticipate the forever relationship we will have in heaven with the God of the living. The difference between hope and despair is knowing the God of the living! That is what will keep us from being sad-you-see (especially at our own funeral)!

Boil It Down For Me

One of the scribes came and heard them arguing, and recognizing that He had answered them well, asked Him, "What commandment is the foremost of all?" Jesus answered, "The foremost is, 'HEAR, O ISRAEL! THE LORD OUR GOD IS ONE LORD; AND YOU SHALL LOVE THE LORD YOUR GOD WITH ALL YOUR HEART, AND WITH ALL YOUR SOUL, AND WITH ALL YOUR MIND, AND WITH ALL YOUR STRENGTH.' The second is this, 'YOU SHALL LOVE YOUR NEIGHBOR AS YOURSELF.' There is no other commandment greater than these." The scribe said to Him, "Right, Teacher; You have truly stated that HE IS ONE, AND THERE IS NO ONE ELSE BESIDES HIM; AND TO LOVE HIM WITH ALL THE HEART AND WITH ALL THE UNDERSTANDING AND WITH ALL THE STRENGTH, AND TO LOVE ONE'S NEIGHBOR AS HIMSELF, is much more than all burnt offerings and sacrifices." When Jesus saw that he had answered intelligently, He said to him, "You are not far from the kingdom of God." After that, no one would venture to ask Him any more questions.

MARK 12:28–34

❦

IT SEEMS ONE of the Scribes was ready to listen. This particular Scribe must have known the Scriptures well and had given much thought to the importance of God's commandments. He seemed to appreciate the teaching of Jesus and wanted to hear His answer to what must have been a much discussed question, "What commandment is the foremost of all?" *What does it all boil down to? If I were to summarize the Law and the Prophets, as a teacher of the Law, how would I do it?*

According to Jesus, it all comes down to loving God and loving people . . . in that order. The first and foremost loving relationship in a person's life is the one between him and his Creator. There must be a recognition of God as the One and only God in our lives. No one and nothing is to come before Him. Recognizing that there is one God and that He is our first priority in love and life is not just a nice thought that needs our consideration, however. It is a commandment that needs our obedience! Complete and full obedience is seen in the all-encompassing scope of "heart, soul, mind, and strength." These four aspects of our life speak to our affections (heart), beliefs (soul), thoughts (mind), and actions (strength).

What is sin if it is not ultimately a shifting of our *affections* away from God and directing them to things and people? What is sin if it is not, when all is said and done, *believing* our soul can live and flourish apart from its Creator? What is sin if it is not deliberately setting our *thoughts* on "things below," thus missing the mark of purity of thought? What is sin if it is not physically acting up and acting out in rebellion? Our rebellious deeds are merely the mess on the inside working its way to the outside. Jesus' command for us to love God with our whole being takes care of both our inside and outside.

Love for God is not a warm sentiment that simply appreciates all He does for us. Love for God is a dangerous and oftentimes uncomfortable journey of setting aside what our flesh cries out for, and answering the call to obey what the Spirit of God within us longs to do. Jesus laid it out for us when He said, "If you love Me, you will keep My commandments" (John 14:15).

For those of us who love to have things "boiled down" (not watered down) for clarity and understanding, Jesus has come through for us. If we concentrate on our primary purpose in life, which is to love God, we will not miss the joy that comes from the many wonderful, if not "dangerous," encounters with Him. If we concentrate on loving God in the all-encompassing scope lined out, we will be able to obey the second great commandment, which is to love the people around us.

How encouraging that the Scribe was able to gain understanding in this. How wonderful that Jesus was able to announce that he was not far from the kingdom of God ... the kingdom where love for God and people is the priority. Let's ask ourselves the hard question now: *Are we loving God with our whole heart, soul, mind, and strength? If not, why not? What is getting in the way of that*

first and foremost command? When we boil it all down, are we
ready to obey the greatest commandment, which is to love God?

More Than Simply A Son

And Jesus [began] to say, as He taught in the temple,
"How [is it that] the scribes say that the Christ is the son
of David? David himself said in the Holy Spirit, 'THE
LORD SAID TO MY LORD, "SIT AT MY RIGHT HAND, UNTIL I
PUT YOUR ENEMIES BENEATH YOUR FEET."' David himself
calls Him 'Lord'; so in what sense is He his son?" And the
large crowd enjoyed listening to Him.

MARK 12:35–37

❦

WITH A SIMPLE yet profound rhetorical question, Jesus was able to
move the crowd closer to a meaningful and significant understanding of His true identity. The time for His betrayal and crucifixion
was drawing ever closer. The people were about to see His frailty
as a human displayed in a truly graphic and disturbing way. He was
about to suffer.

By quoting Psalm 110, Jesus took them to the passage in which
King David called the Messiah his "Lord." That beautiful song, written by David under the power of the Holy Spirit, paid homage to
the Messiah who would one day rule over the world with righteous
justice. Enemies would be defeated and subdued, and the King of
kings would sit upon His rightful throne. While the Psalm made
mention of the suffering the King would cause by way of punishment of His enemies, there was no mention of His own suffering.
David gave us the picture of our Messiah seated at God's right hand
while He subdued the enemies of the King.

So then how was it that the teachers of the Law (the Scribes)
called the Messiah "the son of David"? Jesus seems to imply, with
His rhetorical question, that the teachers of the Law were limiting
the scope of the coming Deliverer's identity by saying that He was
simply the son of David. Their view of Him as a physical descen-
dant of David was only half right. The Messiah's Davidic sonship

was a common Jewish understanding that came straight from the inspired pages of the Old Testament. Blind Bartimaeus knew that the Messiah would come from the family of David and that He would bring mercy with Him. Don't forget his desperate cry, "Jesus, Son of David, have mercy on me!"

Jesus, in His teaching time in the temple, was giving the answer to His own question. The Messiah is both the son of David (man) and the Lord of David (God). The Messiah is God with skin on. The Messiah came in the humility of human flesh in order to die a substitutionary death. The Messiah conquered death with divine power and was seated at the right hand (place of utmost honor) of the Father.

Let's draw close to the Messiah who chose to identify with the pain and suffering of our own humanity. Let's sit at His feet as He teaches. Just because the crowd "enjoyed" His teaching does not mean they received it. Let's do more than enjoy His teaching, let's follow it. We have a chance, this very day, to draw comfort from the Messiah who knows the pain of living as a human, while at the same time submitting our wills to the Messiah who is King of kings. If King David was willing to submit to Him as Lord, would it not seem right for you and me to submit to Him as well?

Style Versus Substance

In His teaching He was saying: "Beware of the scribes who like to walk around in long robes, and [like] respectful greetings in the market places, and chief seats in the synagogues and places of honor at banquets, who devour widows' houses, and for appearance's sake offer long prayers; these will receive greater condemnation."

MARK 12:38–40

❧

JESUS WARNED HIS listeners to beware of Scribes who say one thing in their teaching and act a different way in their living. Long and fancy robes do not make the man spiritual. Demanding respect without earning respect is uncalled for. Needing the best seat in the synagogue and at supper feeds one's ego rather than satisfying the spiritual needs of the people. Of this, Jesus warned, beware.

Beware of who you listen to and who you model your life after. If the highest someone will shoot for is to be well dressed and well addressed, then he has nothing of substance and value to teach us. Their hollow and shallow selves are revealed by their actions. The actions of the teachers of the Law give them away. They take the money (devour the homes) of widows, and yet cover up the crime with long prayers that appear spiritual. It is this very "style versus substance" that should raise the red flag for us.

Consider your own life in light of this warning against and rebuke of hypocrisy. Hypocrisy occurs when the *exterior* actions of our lives do not match our *interior* belief. Hypocrisy is a word that comes from the world of the theater. It is a picture of "acting" on stage. Playing a part that is not really us. The teachers of the Law were putting on a mask, so to speak, in order to take advantage of people for their own self-advancement. Garments, greetings, and greed drove these people to take advantage of those they were supposed to serve. This kind of life is in stark contrast with the life of the poor widow Jesus was about to point out to His listeners.

Followers of Christ are not perfect. Falling to temptation, stumbling in sin, and even blatant rebellion does not necessarily equate to hypocrisy. The world around us watches for that sort of thing and is quick to label believers as hypocrites, but this is not what Jesus was warning against. Jesus was warning against *faking*, not *failing*.

The important thing for us today is to consider the substance of our faith versus the style of our religious actions. Our religious actions can have an acceptable appearance, and yet have nothing to do with a substantive faith. Our faith in Christ is what produces genuine fruit of the Spirit which "works" for the benefit of God's Kingdom. Faith in the power of Christ to infuse us with His life and the commitment to letting that power move us along are God's desires for us. It is what will keep us in close and genuine fellowship with Him. It is what will keep us from *faking* it!

The scribes knew the Law, but refused to know Christ. The scribes, from all appearances, were religious, but lacked a relationship with God. Jesus gave a clear warning to beware of that hypocrisy. Jesus offers us the substance of faith and calls us to reject the mere outward style or form of religion. Consider where we are with this warning. Are we more about style (garments, greetings, and greed) or substance (faith in Christ)? Answering this important question will help us move forward in our relationship with Christ as we abandon the emptiness of religion.

Painful Commitment To God

And He sat down opposite the treasury, and [began] observing how the people were putting money into the treasury; and many rich people were putting in large sums. A poor widow came and put in two small copper coins, which amount to a cent. Calling His disciples to Him, He said to them, "Truly I say to you, this poor widow put in more than all the contributors to the treasury; for they all put in out of their surplus, but she, out of her poverty, put in all she owned, all she had to live on."

MARK 12:41–44

No ONE HAS ever said that following Jesus would be easy. As a matter of fact, Jesus often warned His friends that it would take a commitment to God that would be painful most of the time. He illustrated this point by drawing their attention to a very poor widow who demonstrated her commitment to her Creator with a gift that no doubt "hurt" her pocketbook. She emptied her purse out of a heart full of love for God.

The fact of the matter is that we will either approach God in the giving of our resources (money as well as talents) out of our "surplus" and avoid the pain, or out of our "poverty" where the pain is real and intense. Among the many lessons from the passage, one that must be noted is that God is not impressed with large gifts to Christian ministries and congregations. What is so impressive to God about a million dollars? Rich people giving large sums of money do not impress God. God is pleased with the depth of one's commitment to *Him*, not with the amount of one's philanthropic dabblings.

When you and I give back to God some of what He has entrusted to us (this is not just about money) with an eye toward staying comfortable, we have missed the point. Jesus drew attention to a poor widow who was living a desperately dependent life. She was dependent on God for her daily bread. There was no investment portfolio or 401(k) for her to turn to. She was a woman living in physical poverty, yet in a spiritual sense she was more wealthy than the people entrusted with the spiritual leadership of the whole nation of Israel. She actually gave more, in the eyes of God, by giving two small copper coins out of her poverty than if a wealthy person gave a whole copper mine out of his surplus.

What does this mean for you and me? It means we must do some serious soul searching when it comes to our commitment to God and His mission to advance His kingdom on earth as it is in heaven. The ad campaign slogan, "No pain, no gain" is never truer than in the context of our faith journeys. In a world where people are self-medicating because they want to avoid pain at all costs, no wonder this message about a painful commitment to God gets pushed aside. To limit our involvement in God's work by locking into a particular percentage of giving (tithers beware!) may be settling for a certain comfort zone that has never been sanctioned by God.

When Jesus said, ". . . for where your treasure is, there your heart will be also" (Matthew 6:21), He was giving us a way to gauge our commitment to God's priorities. One of the best gauges for determining our priorities is our checkbook registers. They tell the story of the pursuit of comfort or the pursuit of God. Giving from our surpluses smokes us out as philanthropic dabblers rather than radical followers of Jesus who give "until it hurts," knowing He will take care of us.

No one ever said that following Jesus would be easy. If we are not willing to feel the pain in our pocketbooks, chances are we are not willing to feel the pain in other areas of our faith journey as well. But again, this is not just about money. This is about a painful commitment to God that manifests itself in the giving of everything we *are*, as well as everything we *have*. Whether that is a copper coin or a copper mine is up to each individual.

A Time To Tear Down

As He was going out of the temple, one of His disciples
said to Him, "Teacher, behold what wonderful stones and
what wonderful buildings!" And Jesus said to him, "Do you
see these great buildings? Not one stone will be left upon
another which will not be torn down."

MARK 13:1–2

THE DISCIPLES WERE admiring the architecture and craftsmanship
of the temple and wanted to see if Jesus was equally impressed with
the work of those who invested their time and talent to build it.
Jesus never said whether He was impressed or not, but He did say,
in effect, *take a good look at it now because it will not be around much
longer.* He told them that one day there would be a tearing down of
that with which they were personally impressed.

The prediction made by Jesus capped off His earlier condemnation of the religious leaders' misuse of the temple, as they allowed the ripping off of the "little guys." Jesus predicted the future
destruction of the temple. The pride of the religious leaders, who
placed themselves in a position to "lord it over" people rather than
in a position of service to people, was showing up in the boasts and
brags of those who were impressed with their ability to build such
big and beautiful buildings. Large polished stones, placed perfectly
on top of one another as they towered over the city, spoke of the
genius of man and his ability to build. Should we be impressed
with ourselves? Is God impressed?

This passage is forcing us to ask ourselves some very difficult
questions. One is whether or not we have spent our time building
"stuff" that will not last rather than investing in that which will.
Another question is whether or not we are caught up in pride.
These questions are not just about the time spent building our own
little kingdoms or temples and the pride that develops from that.

They are also about the false sense of security that develops when we are surrounded by our own accomplishments.

Anything and everything built by man will one day be torn down or destroyed, whereas anything and everything built by God will remain. This includes our very lives. "Unless the LORD builds the house, they labor in vain who build it . . ." (Psalm 127:1). The things we build remind us of how smart and industrious we are. They are a sign of what we can do when we buckle down and apply ourselves. Strong and tall buildings must prove how capable we are, right? The danger in this is that we start to believe we can build a life apart from God. We can easily go about building our lives on our own because we are able-bodied men and women with vision, passion, and drive. Success at laying stone upon stone, so to speak, can easily go to our heads. The Lord warns us that such monuments to self will one day be destroyed.

What have you built (or are you currently building) that has subtly become your monument to self? One of the greatest "wake up calls" some people have received from God is the "tearing down" of those monuments. Our skills and abilities to build need to be celebrated as gifts from God, but must not be used to advance our own kingdoms. Our God-given resources and talents must be used to advance the Kingdom of God.

According to the book of Ecclesiastes, there is a time to build up and a time to tear down. Let's be sure that what we build is built in the Lord and not in the flesh. If not, we will be sorely disappointed when we see it all in ruins. We will see our impressive work destroyed in a heap of smoke and ruin. If we want to be truly impressed, let's be impressed with the work of God in our lives, lives that will never be destroyed because the One who built them . . . built them well.

Beginning of Birth Pangs

As He was sitting on the Mount of Olives opposite the temple, Peter and James and John and Andrew were questioning Him privately, "Tell us, when will these things be, and what [will be] the sign when all these things are going to be fulfilled?" And Jesus began to say to them, "See to it that no one misleads you. Many will come in My name, saying, 'I am [He!]' and will mislead many. When you hear of wars and rumors of wars, do not be frightened; [those things] must take place; but [that is] not yet the end. For nation will rise up against nation, and kingdom against kingdom; there will be earthquakes in various places; there will [also] be famines. These things are [merely] the beginning of birth pangs."

MARK 13:3–8

WITH A SMALL audience of four, Jesus conducted some Q&A right after He shared the shocking news that the temple would one day be destroyed. The first and foremost question was, *When? When will this happen and what will be the signs? What will tip us off?* The words of Christ as recorded in Mark 13 were words meant for the warning and encouragement of His disciples (in their lifetime), as well as believers in the years to come (including you and me). Some of what Jesus spoke of in the future tense has already happened. Some of what He shared has yet to take place. All of what He said is for you and me.

He made it clear that imposters would spring up as nation goes to war against nation. Not only will countries fight each other (wars), but also the earth will fight itself (earthquakes). A deteriorating world will signal the end. Don't be deceived in the midst of the pain, Jesus warned. With God, nothing is left to chance and His people are not left to fend for themselves. Christ gave them and us enough detail regarding how it all ends so that we would not worry while we watch.

Fakes, fighting, and *famine* will be the signs that the end is near. While the world has seen all three of these—even before the time of Christ's first advent—Jesus was saying that these will increase in number and intensity as the end draws near, just as birth pangs increase in number and intensity.

It was reported in 1992 that a group of academics and historians compiled this startling information: since 3600 BC, the world has known only 292 years of peace! During this period there have been 14,351 wars, large and small, in which 3.64 billion people have been killed. The value of the property destroyed is equal to a golden belt around the world 97.2 miles wide and 33 feet thick. Since 650 BC, there have also been 1,656 arms races, only 16 of which have not ended in war. Only 292 years of peace in a span of 5,500 years is not good news at all.

The good news is, however, that Christ is not going to leave His Church here on earth through the events that follow the "birth pangs." Though we will see the world continue to deteriorate in the area of *fakes, fighting,* and *famine,* we will not experience the biblical events described as "the Great Tribulation." God has made specific promises (1 Thessalonians 4:13–18) that the Church will be taken up and out just before the Great Tribulation is unleashed on earth. This particular doctrine of the End Times has received a great deal of exposure through the popular *Left Behind* series by Tim LaHaye and Jerry Jenkins. The fact of the matter is that news of wars and rumors of wars will intensify. The number and intensity of famine and earthquakes will rise. We are told that things *will* get worse.

Let's not lose heart as the news around us gets worse and worse. Let's pray for victims of earthquakes as we ignore those who claim to be the returned Christ. We have been told in advance what to watch for. Though the "birth pangs" will increase in number and intensity, they are simply a sign of things to come. In the meantime, let's pray as John, the disciple "whom Jesus loved", prayed many years ago when he prayed, "Come, Lord Jesus" (Revelation 22:20)! The joy of His imminent return will cause us to forget the pain of today's reality just as the joy of birth causes moms around the world to forget the pain of labor. Yes . . . Come, Lord Jesus! Come quickly!

It Won't Be Pretty

"But be on your guard; for they will deliver you to [the] courts, and you will be flogged in [the] synagogues, and you will stand before governors and kings for My sake, as a testimony to them. The gospel must first be preached to all the nations. When they arrest you and hand you over, do not worry beforehand about what you are to say, but say whatever is given you in that hour; for it is not you who speak, but [it is] the Holy Spirit. Brother will betray brother to death, and a father [his] child; and children will rise up against parents and have them put to death. You will be hated by all because of My name, but the one who endures to the end, he will be saved."

MARK 13:9–13

THE PROPHETIC WORDS spoken by Christ in today's passage had in view a "near" as well as a "far" fulfillment. In other words, the disciples realized the reality of His words in their own lives when they were hauled into courts, flogged in synagogues, and forced to defend themselves before governors and kings. Christ warned that people from government, religion, and family would oppose them and persecute them because of their love for Him and their loyalty to Him. To understand the reality of this situation in the life of the disciples, read the rest of the New Testament. It is all there! Jesus' prophecies were fulfilled in the lives of those who first heard them. But the prophecies would have a final and complete fulfillment thousands of years later.

That's right, Jesus' words also have a "far" fulfillment that we have yet to see fully realized. Even though believers all over the world are facing government, religious, and family opposition to their faith, the words of Christ in this passage are yet to be fully realized. Jesus, in His prophetic discourse, was laying out the reality of what will happen to people who become believers *after* the Rapture of the Church (which will be the next prophetic event to take place). Once the Rapture occurs, the Great Tribulation will break out. Those who become followers of Christ in that period of time will face tremendous persecution . . . and it won't be pretty.

Jesus described a time when governments will make it their objective to silence followers of Christ. The period of time will also be marked by religious opposition that will turn violent. Believers will be pressured to recant their faith in Jesus. The encouragement for these suffering followers of Christ is to not worry about what they will say. The promise was made that the words would be personally given to them by the Holy Spirit. Can you imagine the assurance and confidence these precious souls will have when faced with such difficult circumstances? They are promised help from God Himself to answer the hard questions. They are promised that the words will come to them just in the nick of time.

Jesus doesn't soften the message one bit. He continues by describing the assault people will face from brothers, fathers, and children. It won't be teasing and taunting, either. According to Jesus, "Brother will betray brother to death, and a father his child; and children will rise up against parents and have them put to death." Jesus assures us that it won't be pretty. Followers of Christ will be hated simply because they are friends with Jesus. It will be a time when people will have to be very careful who they call friend.

In a sense, we see this kind of opposition to Jesus and His friends today. Government is not only distancing itself from the Christian faith, it is taking steps to oppose the faith. Certain world religions have declared war on all those who do not believe as they do. Families are hating one another simply because Jesus matters to some and not to others.

Let's not lose heart if opposition to our faith gets intense. We know that the Holy Spirit will give us the right words to say at just the right time because the promise made by Christ is for us as well. The assurance from Jesus is that times are tough and will only get tougher. Let's hold on to the promise that He is coming to get those who are His and that there is great reward for those who persevere. While believers are promised a rescue at just the right time, they are reminded to hang in there. God is a very present help and promises to never leave or forsake His own. Even if it gets real ugly!

Seven Years of Death and Deception

"But when you see the ABOMINATION OF DESOLATION standing where it should not be (let the reader understand), then those who are in Judea must flee to the mountains. The one who is on the housetop must not go down, or go in to get anything out of his house; and the one who is in the field must not turn back to get his coat. But woe to those who are pregnant and to those who are nursing babies in those days! But pray that it may not happen in the winter. For those days will be a [time of] tribulation such as has not occurred since the beginning of the creation which God created until now, and never will. Unless the Lord had shortened [those] days, no life would have been saved; but for the sake of the elect, whom He chose, He shortened the days. And then if anyone says to you, 'Behold, here is the Christ'; or, 'Behold, [He is] there'; do not believe [him]; for false Christs and false prophets will arise, and will show signs and wonders, in order to lead astray, if possible, the elect. But take heed; behold, I have told you everything in advance."

MARK 13:14–23

IT COULD VERY well be that once the Church is raptured (taken from the earth) the world will be thrown into tremendous confusion and turmoil. Leaders in key government and military positions will suddenly be gone. A vacuum of leadership will exist in churches, schools, companies, and vital service industries. People who are left behind will be stumped, scared, and scrambling for answers and leadership. It is my opinion that the United States government and military will be deeply impacted by the Rapture and America's ability to protect its own homeland, as well as Israel's, will be compromised. From out of the chaos, a world leader will arise who will be attractive and able to bring calm and coolness to the chaos.

Enter the anti-Christ. Jesus warned that when people see *"the abomination of desolation* standing where it should not be" (emphasis added), they should run for the hills. The "abomination of desolation" is a person. This person will appear safe, but will actually be dangerous and murderous. Speaking primarily, but not exclusively, to the Jews who are left on earth during this time, Jesus was warning that the best way for them to survive the wrath of the new world leader would be to hide in the mountains. There won't be time to go back to the house to pack . . . run! It will be worse for pregnant and nursing moms. Being on the run and in hiding is hard enough when you have to just worry about yourself. To care for a newborn will make it much harder.

Jesus described this coming period of time as "a time of tribulation such as has not occurred since the beginning of the creation which God created. . . ." This means the Holocaust, as horrific as it was, will pale in comparison to this impending doomsday period. The only way it could be worse is if the Lord did not limit the time to the seven years described in Daniel 9:27. These very dark and evil days will be marked by death and deception led by one very deceiving and deadly leader. He will lead the Great Tribulation against God's people.

This passage, though future in its fulfillment, has application for you and me today. We can rest assured that God is a God of His word. His promise in Revelation 3:10 is to keep His Church "from the hour of testing." All believers who are on earth at the time of the Rapture will be kept from the Great Tribulation. While we rejoice in that good news, let's double and triple our efforts to tell our friends and family of the death and destruction that awaits those who are "left behind." Even though people from every tongue and nation will have a chance to trust Christ in the midst of the Tribulation, it will still be a horrific scene that we would not wish on our fiercest enemy, much less our friends.

This is not the time for complacency. The Rapture (and the following Tribulation) could take place today. There are people who are in desperate need of knowing Jesus as the Rescuer of their lost and drifting lives. Let's make sure those we love and work with know the truth about Jesus. He is coming back for His own and there are people who need to know His love and grace. There are people who need to know they don't have to go through the seven horrible years the Bible describes as death and deception. Life and truth are a much better future ... for everyone!

The Return Of The King

"But in those days, after that tribulation, THE SUN WILL BE DARKENED AND THE MOON WILL NOT GIVE ITS LIGHT, AND THE STARS WILL BE FALLING from heaven, and the powers that are in the heavens will be shaken. Then they will see THE SON OF MAN COMING IN CLOUDS with great power and glory. And then He will send forth the angels, and will gather together His elect from the four winds, from the farthest end of the earth to the farthest end of heaven."

MARK 13:24–27

THE HORROR OF the Great Tribulation will be suddenly ended by the return of the King. Jesus not only promised that He was going to prepare a place for us, but that He would return for us and take us to that prepared place (John 14:2–3). This coming for His own is known as the Rapture. The return of the King mentioned in today's passage is known as the Second Coming of Christ. Those who are fighting for their lives in the midst of the seven years of the death and deception known as the Tribulation will have the assurance of the King's return to look forward to.

Something astronomical (literally) will happen in the sky. The sun, moon, and stars will stop being normal, which will cause folks to stop and look up. Once everyone has directed his attention to the skies, he will see the most wonderful and awesome advent in the history of the world. He will witness the powerful return of the King.

For amazing details regarding the majestic return of Christ, read Revelation 19:11–16. The imagery of these verses describes the conquering Messiah coming in truth and power to make things right. Exacting justice, fighting and defeating the evil that has dominated earth for years, and gathering His beloved children cap off

His majestic return.

The King will instruct His angels to do a worldwide sweep of the earth and gather those who trusted Him during the seven year Tribulation. No cave will be unchecked. Every forest will be searched. All beaches will be sifted. Every home emptied and every work place searched. All of God's children will be brought in from the cold. All of those who found their life in Christ after the Rapture will find themselves swept up in the arms of angels as they collect believers from the four corners of the earth. All His children will be brought to Him.

Again, we are reading about what will take place in the future. These words are recorded in Scripture and will be left for those who need to know the truth once the Church is removed. Believers will find hope and comfort in the words of Christ. They will be reassured day after day that the King is coming back for them.

Let's learn to find the same comfort in God's Word today. There are thousands of promises in the pages of our Bibles that go unread and unclaimed. Though what we go through today will not compare to the horror of the future, we still struggle with broken dreams, relationships, hopes, promises, and lives. We suffer from our own sin and the sin of others. What does God's Word say to us in such dark times? The only way to know the promises of God is to read the promises of God. He has made every effort to communicate His heart to us. The King has made every effort to communicate His love for and ultimate protection of those who are rightly related to Him through His Son.

The King will one day ride in on His prodigious white stallion with "great power and glory." In the meantime, let's live our lives in such a way that we reflect that power and glory to a lost and dying world. The King would be very pleased!

Parable of the Rodeo and the Fig Tree

"Now learn the parable from the fig tree: when its branch
has already become tender and puts forth its leaves, you
know that summer is near. Even so, you too, when you see
these things happening, recognize that He is near, [right]
at the door. Truly I say to you, this generation will not
pass away until all these things take place. Heaven and
earth will pass away, but My words will not pass away. But
of that day or hour no one knows, not even the angels in
heaven, nor the Son, but the Father [alone]."

MARK 13:28–32

❧

ASK ANY HOUSTONIAN how he or she knows winter is over and
they will probably answer with one word . . . Rodeo! That's right,
just as there are signs in nature that indicate the coming summer
months, Houston's world famous rodeo lets us know winter is over.
When the rodeo hits town . . . behold, spring has sprung.

Though the disciples did not have the parable of the rodeo to
indicate the change of seasons, they were able to learn from the
parable of the fig tree. When the branches got tender and the leaves
started to form, they knew summer was just around the corner. So
it will be with the signs of the prophetic times. When the world
sees the events described in Mark 13:14–23, they will know it is
all about to end.

Because the Greek word *genea*, which means "generation," can
refer to one's living contemporaries as well as to a group of people
descended from a common ancestor, it is best, in this context, to
understand the word in both senses. In other words, the Jews living
at the time of Christ were in view since they saw the destruction

of Jerusalem and the temple. Jesus also had in mind the group who will be living during the Great Tribulation, and thus seeing the End Time events He described.

The lesson for us today is that we can trust Jesus' words. Though things and events will come to a final end, the Word of God (the words of Christ) will remain forever. Things *did happen* just as Jesus had predicted, and so we can trust that things *will happen* just as He predicted. The Jews of His day saw the temple destroyed (its final end), and there will be a group of Jews (and others) who will see the Tribulation come to its final end. Even when all things cease and desist, the Word of God remains active, accurate, and alive.

Let's take it to heart that you and I can trust Jesus' words. You and I can trust the promises He has made. Heaven and earth *will* pass away, according to the Lord, but His words *will not* pass away! It has been said that the two things that will last forever are the souls of people and the Word of God. Because of this, it would be wise for us to invest our lives heavily in both. All is fleeting except the truth expressed by the Son of God and the souls He created for relationship. A man or woman is no fool to invest his or her life in the two things that will never pass away.

The best way I know to invest in the Word of God is to prayerfully study and apply the truth it contains. We must commit ourselves to obeying the truths we glean from the pages of the Scriptures. They are true and trustworthy. The best way I know to invest in the souls of people is to communicate the truth of the Scriptures in a clear and loving way.

The Lord has told us that heaven and earth will pass away and yet His words will still remain. Let's do all we can to communicate the truth of His words to those who are still here. The "season" seems to be changing. Time may be running out. The "rodeo" is about to start and there are still people who do not know how to get a ticket. Let's be sure they know . . . before it's too late!

Be Alert

"Take heed, keep on the alert; for you do not know when
the [appointed] time will come. [It is] like a man away
on a journey, [who] upon leaving his house and putting
his slaves in charge, [assigning] to each one his task, also
commanded the doorkeeper to stay on the alert. Therefore,
be on the alert—for you do not know when the master of
the house is coming, whether in the evening, at midnight,
or when the rooster crows, or in the morning—in case he
should come suddenly and find you asleep. What I say to
you I say to all, 'Be on the alert!'"

MARK 13:33–37

YEARS AGO, MY brother had a T-shirt that said, "Be alert ... the
world needs more lerts!" To this day, I think about that shirt when I
hear people admonish others to "Be alert!" At the time, I just chuck-
led. I figured his shirt was just funny, not really saying anything
important. Being alert, however, is exactly what Jesus is calling us
to be in these dark and broken days.

There are several reasons to be on guard and aware these days.
One reason, according to the context of today's passage, is that we
are here as servants in the Master's house with our own particular
tasks to accomplish. If we lose focus in our assignment or let down
in our responsibility, there will be regret if the Master returns while
we are being lax. Jesus tells us to consider His return to be imminent. These verses speak about His return for His Church. This
event is known as the Rapture.

The Rapture will be sudden and quick. There will not be time
to "tidy the house" for the Master. There will not be time to make
the bed or vacuum the floor, so to speak, in regards to our lives. It
will all happen in the "twinkling of an eye" (1 Corinthians 15:52).
There will be no time to *start* doing good nor *stop* doing bad. It will

happen quickly. Therefore, we are to be alert.

I don't know about you, but I can't wait for His return. Don't get me wrong! I love my life and all that the Lord has entrusted to me by way of family and ministry . . . but the effects of the darkness and brokenness of this present age sometimes makes me feel defeated. It is in those times of feeling defeated that I have to remember the truth of certain Scriptures. Consider what Paul said when he wrote to the Corinthians, "But we have this treasure in earthen vessels, so that the surpassing greatness of the power will be of God and not from ourselves; we are afflicted in every way, but not crushed; perplexed, but not despairing; persecuted, but not forsaken; struck down, but not destroyed; always carrying about in the body the dying of Jesus, so that the life of Jesus also may be manifested in our body" (2 Corinthians 4:7–10).

It is because of the life of Christ in us that we are never actually defeated. We are down, but not out. We are *feeling* abandoned, but we are never alone. It feels as if the Master has left and will never return, but that is not so. He is standing at the door ready to come back. But are we ready for His return? Are we alert as Christ commanded?

My hope and prayer is that He will return soon. My fear is that He will return while I am in a state of "sleepy spirituality," not being what He has called me to be and not doing what He has called me to do. Worse yet, doing something He has called me not to do.

Being alert is what Christ calls us to be. This makes me think He knew the world would always need more lerts! Maybe my brother's T-shirt really did say something important.

Treacherous Tuesday

Now the Passover and Unleavened Bread were two days away; and the chief priests and the scribes were seeking how to seize Him by stealth and kill [Him]; for they were saying, "Not during the festival, otherwise there might be a riot of the people."

MARK 14:1–2

THE TREACHEROUS PLOT to overtake Jesus and stop His tremendous momentum by killing Him was hatched two days before the Passover feast would be celebrated. The Passover meal was going to be on a Thursday; therefore, we know this plan was hatched on a Tuesday. That day will forever go down in my heart and mind as "Treacherous Tuesday."

I was amazed at the controversy that swirled around Mel Gibson's movie, *The Passion of the Christ.* In interviews broadcast around the world, he was forced to answer the question, *Are you anti-Semitic?* The reason the question was asked is because the film portrays Jesus suffering under the authority of the Jewish leaders. Some people feel the film blames the Jews for the death of Jesus. Diane Sawyer asked Mel Gibson, "Who killed Jesus?"

According to today's passage, two days before the Passover, the chief priests and scribes hatched the treacherous plot to kill Jesus. It is important to note the timing because they were afraid to arrest Him during the festival for fear the crowds would riot. The plan that was hatched in secret had to be carried out in secret lest the people revolt. It seems that treachery is very much at home in the dark and secret places of men's hearts.

I cannot speak to the dark and secret places of men's hearts without including my own. I happen to agree with Mel Gibson's answer to Diane Sawyer's question. He responded, "I killed Jesus." The darkness of my own sin and rebellion has hatched thousands of Treacherous Tuesdays. My own fear of "the crowd" has sent me into the plotting mode time and time again. Plotting how to marginalize Jesus has become an art form in my life. I continually feel the pressure of His Deity and authority in my life and find myself pushing Him away with my own self-will and independence. As hard as it is to admit, these passages are about the darkness and treachery of my own heart. It mentions the chief priests and scribes, but it is really about me.

In testimony to the love and grace of God, I was told years ago that if I were the only person on earth, Jesus still would have come to earth to die for me. His love for me is so deep and real that He would have come to die on the cross just for me. This is not a testimony of how "worthy" I am, but rather a testimony of how loving and gracious God is. I found great comfort in those words for years, and then something very sobering dawned on me.

If I were the only one on earth, then it would have fallen to me to betray Him. It would have been me tying His hands behind His back and hauling Him to jail. I would be the one to whip Him, beat Him, spit on Him, mock Him, laugh at Him, and yes . . . hate Him. Someone would have to kill Jesus in order for Him to become the ultimate sacrifice for sin, and that someone would have to be me. I killed Jesus.

The Scripture puts us all *on* the hook for the death of Jesus. Though the dark and treacherous conversation that put the plan in motion was originally between some unnamed priests and scribes, I know deep down in my heart that I would have fit into that conversation really well. There have been too many Treacherous Tuesdays in my life to try to deny it. Mel Gibson seems to believe that for himself, as well. I only wish he could know he doesn't own those himself. I own Treacherous Tuesday with him.

A Love That Saturates

While He was in Bethany at the home of Simon the leper, and reclining [at the table], there came a woman with an alabaster vial of very costly perfume of pure nard; [and] she broke the vial and poured it over His head. But some were indignantly [remarking] to one another, "Why has this perfume been wasted? For this perfume might have been sold for over three hundred denarii, and [the money] given to the poor." And they were scolding her. But Jesus said, "Let her alone; why do you bother her? She has done a good deed to Me. For you always have the poor with you, and whenever you wish you can do good to them; but you do not always have Me. She has done what she could; she has anointed My body beforehand for the burial. Truly I say to you, wherever the gospel is preached in the whole world, what this woman has done will also be spoken of in memory of her."

MARK 14:3–9

❦

To SHOW THE sharp contrast between the warm-hearted love of Mary and the cold-hearted betrayal of Judas toward Jesus, Mark inserts this narrative. Mark does not record this event in strict chronological order, the way John did in his gospel, so that he could draw attention to an important theme. The theme of love versus hatred for Jesus is highlighted here, and we are called to find ourselves in the story.

While attending a festive dinner at the home of Simon, a man apparently cured of leprosy by Jesus, an unnamed woman (we know it is Mary, the sister of Martha and Lazarus, by referring to John's gospel account) breaks open an expensive bottle of perfume and saturates Jesus' head with it. Several important elements characterize this act of love. Each characteristic must be considered in our own approach to Jesus.

First of all, our love for Jesus must cause us to *stoop* as Mary's caused her to *stoop*. You see, Jesus was reclining at a very low table in Simon's home. He was lying down while propping Himself up on His elbow. Mary would have had to "bend a knee" in order to get close enough to Jesus' head. It was Mary's love for Jesus that allowed her to set her pride aside and *stoop*. Let's consider our own willingness to set our pride aside in our relationship with Jesus. Love for Jesus will bring about a bended knee of submission to His heart and will. It shows we love Him more than we love ourselves. A stooping love is an honorable love.

Secondly, our love for Jesus will be *sacrificial*, as Mary's was. She gave up a jar of very expensive perfume for the sake of Jesus. The perfume was worth a full year's salary. Let's consider our own willingness to make sacrifices out of our love for Jesus. Sacrifices in the area of time, talent, and treasure should be considered on a daily basis. Jesus is worth all we have. Giving our time, talent, and treasure out of love for Jesus is a very practical way of showing sacrificial affection for Him. Mary has modeled this sacrificial love for us very well. Let's follow her lead.

Thirdly, our love for Jesus must be *saturating*. Just as *all* of the perfume was poured out and saturated the head of Christ, our love must be extravagant and saturating. The love in our heart for Jesus must be poured out without measure. No holding back. No diverting it to other people or objects. Jesus deserves all our love. It is only out of a proper loving relationship with Jesus that we will have anything to offer friends, family, and neighbors in the way of godly love. Just as Mary's love was saturating, ours must be as well.

Lastly, our love must push through the *suffering* as Mary's did. She had a group of thugs scolding her for her actions. She was accused of wastefulness. There are going to be many times in our journeys of faith that we will be accused of wasting our lives on Jesus. People will ridicule us and reject us for our love and devotion to Christ. We must, however, not lose heart. Jesus stands ready to defend us, as He did Mary.

Our love for Jesus will cause us to bend the knee of pride and *stoop* in humble submission. Our love for Christ will move us to *sacrifice* our time, talent, and treasure. Our love must be *saturating* and we must be ready to *suffer* for our love. The story of Mary's love for Jesus is told today just as He promised. This tells us that a love for God that *saturates* is talked about for generation after generation. For how long do you think the story of your love for Jesus will be told?

Selling Out

Then Judas Iscariot, who was one of the twelve, went off
to the chief priests in order to betray Him to them. They
were glad when they heard [this], and promised to give
him money. And he [began] seeking how to betray Him at
an opportune time.

MARK 14:10–11

❧

THE COLD-HEARTED BETRAYAL on the part of Judas Iscariot is in
stark contrast to the warm-hearted love of Mary. While Mary
stooped to saturate His head with perfume, Judas took steps to
stab Him in the back.

Judas reported to the chief priests his willingness to give Christ
up to them. He told them he would inform them of His movements
and tell them the best time and place to arrest Him apart from the
notice of the growing crowds. His willingness to take money for
this act of treacherous treason is legendary. While Mary was emp-
tying her purse for Christ, Judas was padding his own.

Judas was not a believer. Judas was a man who looked only to
his own interests. His hopes for material and political gain were
dashed as he realized Jesus was not going to establish a political
kingdom. As the only one of the twelve not from Galilee, he may
have been responding to the official notice (John 11:57) to have
Jesus turned over to the authorities. All he needed was an opportune time.

Technically speaking, a believer cannot be a "Judas." Believers
can (and often do) find themselves denying Christ as Peter did, but
the "heart" of a "Judas" is unique to non-believers. While believers
can't *be* a "Judas," they can certainly *act like* a "Judas."

Let's face it, even believers struggle with deep disappointment
with God. We expect Him to "come through" for us. A fleshly desire to gain materially, rather than spiritually can bring out a lot of

Judas-like behavior in us all. Most of us look at Judas with deep disgust. Most us of are scandalized by his betrayal. All of us, however, must be honest with ourselves when it comes to our own "betrayal" of Jesus. Too often, our deep disappointment with God sends us out looking to make a deal with the world. It may not be "thirty pieces of silver" that we accept for our treason, but there are a lot more things we are willing to take in exchange.

Cutting a deal with the world, or selling out, can take on different looks. Spiritual treason shows up in our willingness to accept the deceit of sin over the truth of God's will for our lives. It shows up in our frequent, if not prolonged, wanderings through the desert of indulgences. Eugene Peterson's translation on Galatians 5 paints the ugly picture quite well. He writes, "It is obvious what kind of life develops out of trying to get your own way all the time: repetitive, loveless, cheap sex; a stinking accumulation of mental and emotional garbage; frenzied and joyless grabs for happiness; trinket gods; magic-show religion; paranoid loneliness; cutthroat competition; all-consuming-yet-never-satisfied wants; a brutal temper; an impotence to love and be loved; divided homes and divided lives; small-minded and lopsided pursuits; the vicious habit of depersonalizing everyone into a rival; uncontrolled and uncontrollable addictions; ugly parodies of community. I could go on."

Let's be sure we don't sell out to the world by turning on Jesus for our own "thirty pieces of silver." Treason is treacherous enough for someone who says he loves Jesus but really doesn't. The treachery stings even more when the treason comes from those who really do love Him.

Furnished and Ready

On the first day of Unleavened Bread, when the Passover
[lamb] was being sacrificed, His disciples said to Him,
"Where do You want us to go and prepare for You to
eat the Passover?" And He sent two of His disciples and
said to them, "Go into the city, and a man will meet you
carrying a pitcher of water; follow him; and wherever he
enters, say to the owner of the house, 'The Teacher says,
"Where is My guest room in which I may eat the Passover
with My disciples?"' And he himself will show you a large
upper room furnished [and] ready; prepare for us there."
The disciples went out and came to the city, and found [it]
just as He had told them; and they prepared the Passover.

MARK 14:12–16

THE EVENTS OF this passage are very similar to what happened
when the disciples secured the colt on which Jesus rode into town
(cf. Mark 11:1–6). While this passage certainly reinforces the fact
that Jesus had supernatural knowledge, it speaks more to the fact
that there are people in the world whose lives are "furnished and
ready" for the Messiah.

There was a tremendous need for security at this point in Jesus'
ministry. It seems that He arranged with a friend in Jerusalem to
have the Passover meal at his home. In order to keep the location a
secret, a plan was devised to communicate the location at just the
right time. A man (most likely a servant) carrying a water jar would
be the signal. They were to follow him to the undisclosed location
and ask the owner about the "guest room." The fact that the owner
himself would show the way was an important confirming fact.

Consider for a moment the qualities of the homeowner. In the
midst of growing opposition to Jesus by religious and government
officials, he was willing to risk his own life and property by hosting

the supper. The owner's *faith* in Jesus pushed him past any fear that may have tried to thwart his devotion. For you and me to have a "home" (our life) furnished and ready for Jesus, we must continually give attention to our faith. Our faith is a muscle that only grows strong with use. Our faith in Christ as God's Messiah will push us past any fear that may try to thwart our commitment.

Another quality to consider is *generosity*. It seems the house was given over for Christ's use with nothing held back. The owner was not stingy with his home. The large upper room was furnished and ready without grumbling and complaining. The room was offered with such opened hands, so to speak, that Jesus confidently called it His when He instructed the disciples to ask, on His behalf, "Where is *My* guest room ..."(emphasis added). A generous heart says to God, "My house is your house." How are you doing in this area of your life? Do you see possessions as yours, or do they belong to God? The biblical view of possessions is that you and I are stewards of what belongs to God. A generous heart gives back to God what is rightfully His.

One last quality to consider is *servanthood*. The owner of the home served the Lord by working to make the room ready. He made sure it was furnished and ready for thirteen hungry men. The man arranged, swept, dusted, aired out, furnished, and readied the room for a traditionally festive meal. It would have taken a real servant's heart to make a large room like that ready.

Let's consider the condition of our *faith* right now. Are we growing in our faith in such a way that fear does not paralyze us? Let's consider the depth of our *generosity*. Do we consider what we possess to be His or ours? What about *servanthood*? Are we working to make our hearts "furnished and ready" for Him?

Faith, generosity, and *servanthood* are three qualities to consider as we continue to arrange, sweep, dust, air out, furnish, and ready our hearts for Jesus. Let's all be ready to say to Jesus, "*Mi casa es su casa!* My house is your house!"

Trust or Turn

When it was evening He came with the twelve. As they were reclining [at the table] and eating, Jesus said, "Truly I say to you that one of you will betray Me—one who is eating with Me." They began to be grieved and to say to Him one by one, "Surely not I?" And He said to them, "[It is] one of the twelve, one who dips with Me in the bowl. For the Son of Man [is to] go just as it is written of Him; but woe to that man by whom the Son of Man is betrayed! [It would have been] good for that man if he had not been born."

MARK 14:17–21

IN THE MIDST of the festive Passover meal, Jesus interrupts with really bad news. The news was hard to hear because it was so shocking. The news of betrayal sent each disciple scrambling for clarity. Each disciple started questioning his own loyalty.

The fact that each one said to Him, "Surely not I?" is a clear indication they all (one by one) saw the potential inside them to turn on Jesus. None was so naïve as to think he was above failure. Each one grieved at the announcement because each one knew he had it in himself to turn on Jesus.

At that particular moment, none of the disciples vehemently denied the possibility of turning on Christ. Peter would later fight the prediction of his own failure, but each disciple responded with Christ's prediction with the question, *Is it I?* Each of them knew the spirit in him was willing to stay loyal, but that the flesh was weak.

As we think about what may have actually been going on at the time, we may need to admit that Judas may not have been the only one having intense feelings of disappointment with Jesus. They all, to some degree, had hoped Jesus was going to set up a political kingdom with them filling the choice cabinet seats. The question we must all answer, as the disciples did, is *What am I going to do with my disappointment with God?*

There are two basic options for each of us: *trust* or *turn*. When God does not "come through" for us, will we *trust* Him or will we *turn* on Him? If we were going to be truly humble and honest, we would have to admit we are capable of both. Trusting God, even when He supposedly lets us down, is what our journey of faith is about. Turning on God because He supposedly disappoints us is a sign of a "fair-weather" friend. Will we bless God only if He lives up to our selfish expectations? Will we turn from God at the very moment we realize He is not putting our desires before His? Are we going to be His friend at breakfast and His foe at dinner?

Consider the agenda you have been taking to God lately. Have your prayers of petition been absent of the important phrase, ". . . yet not my will, but Yours be done"? If not, you could be setting yourself up for deep disappointment with God. An intimate relationship with God comes when His creation gets in line with Him by submitting heart, soul, mind, and strength in love and devotion. Intimacy with God does not happen when the creation tries to manipulate the Creator into line.

The believer's heart has the ability to trust God even when things don't go his or her way. The new nature of a child of God is able to stay faithful to his or her Father. The old nature is the one that continues to struggle with not getting its way. Living according to the Spirit produces a life that trusts God even in the midst of deep disappointment. Living according to the flesh produces a life that will turn on God when that deep disappointment develops.

The potential to turn on God is in all of us. The potential to trust, however, is there as well. Disappointment with God will develop in our lives many times over the years to come. The question still remains—will we *trust* or will we *turn*?

Provision and Promise

While they were eating, He took [some] bread, and after a blessing He broke [it], and gave [it] to them, and said, "Take [it]; this is My body." And when He had taken a cup [and] given thanks, He gave [it] to them, and they all drank from it. And He said to them, "This is My blood of the covenant, which is poured out for many. Truly I say to you, I will never again drink of the fruit of the vine until that day when I drink it new in the kingdom of God."

MARK 14:22–25

THE PASSOVER MEAL (Jesus' last supper before dying) consisted of roasted lamb and unleavened bread. There were wine, bitter herbs, and a sauce made of dried fruit mixed with wine, vinegar, and spices. Jesus was thankful for the plate of food set before Him, even though everything on the plate reminded Him of His calling to sacrifice His life for sinners.

Jesus was celebrating the Passover meal with men whom He had created for an intimate relationship. The intended spiritual connection for which they were created was broken due to their sin. The lamb on Jesus' plate represented the bridge that would soon be built between God and His wayward creation. The lamb on His plate represented Him. The meal He found Himself eating alongside His friends was punctuated with bitter herbs. The bitter herbs were a part of the meal in order to remind participants of Israel's bitter experience in the desert. The unleavened bread represented both the spiritual purity of the Messiah and the spiritual purity that can be ours through the Messiah.

Jesus took time during the meal to give a visual lesson to His friends. The bread and the wine represented His body and His blood. His broken body and His poured out blood were the materials used by God to build a bridge between Him and His fallen children. His broken body and poured out blood provided Him an opportunity to make a *provision* and a *promise*.

First the *provision*. His words "take it" show that He is the great Giver. He was providing a way back to Himself. He was providing the solution to man's horrible dilemma that is spiritual at its core. Only in His broken body and poured out blood could the impasse, caused by sin, be conquered. You and I cannot get past our sin and its consequences without God's provision of grace. God's grace was provided through the "paschal lamb." The Hebrew word from which we get our word "paschal" means to *leap over*, figuratively, *to spare, to show mercy,* and denotes an "overstepping." This means the paschal sacrifice effected the "passing over" of God's judgment of sin. His provision is His grace by virtue of the breaking of Jesus' body on the cross and the subsequent resurrection. This would be a good time to consider whether you have received His provision. He is saying to us, "Take it." Have we?

Now the *promise*. Jesus made a promise that He would not drink of the "fruit of the vine" until the day He drinks it new in the kingdom of God. This promise gives us the hope of a wonderful future with Him. The resurrection of Christ means He is alive today. His promise is to return for us and set us at His banquet table. It will be at that wonderful table that He will raise a cup full of the "fruit of the vine" once again. Think about it this way: at the last supper, He raised the cup looking *toward* His death. At the great banquet feast that awaits us, He will raise the cup looking *back* at His death.

The *provision* of forgiveness (to spare or show mercy) has been made. Have you taken it? The *promise* to drink the cup new in the kingdom of God has also been made. Are you counting on it? A person's past can be erased by the forgiveness provided in the paschal lamb while his future can be secured by the promise of His return. He has said, "Take it." Let me ask you this . . . have you?

A Song In The Night

After singing a hymn, they went out to the Mount of
Olives.

MARK 14:26

❧

THE PASSOVER MEAL started with the singing of Hallel (praise)
Psalms. Two or more groups of people that gathered around the
table would sing alternate sections of the Psalms. A traditional
Passover meal would include the singing of Psalms 113 to 118. The
first two of these were sung to start things off and the remaining
four were sung at the end of the meal. Keep this in mind the next
time you read Psalm 118. More than likely, it is the song Jesus sang
in the night . . . just before He was betrayed and murdered.

It is amazing to me that Christ sat with His friends singing
songs of praise knowing what was coming His way. If it were me,
to be quite honest, I would probably have been focused on *myself*
and all the "doom and gloom" I was feeling in the night, rather than
focused on the Lord. Jesus was about to go through what is, in my
opinion, the most horrific torture devised by man. He was going
to be beaten and flogged to such a degree that His flesh would be
hanging off His back. He was about to feel the most alone a human
being can possibly feel. It was a very dark night for Him and it was
going to get darker.

All of us find ourselves in "darkness" at times. Our calamity and
misery may not be exactly like Jesus', but it hurts nonetheless. The
pain of loneliness is just as real for those who are told they will be
loved to the very end, and yet end up abandoned and alone. The
misery associated with illness can embitter people without much
notice or warning. Fear paralyzes the masses to the point of despair,
and yet the symptoms go unchecked.

The author of Psalm 77 was going through a miserable time
in his life. He was finding himself oppressed by the darkness. He

was having a hard time hearing the Lord in the midst of the pain. He then did something that brought him a moment of great hope and joy. He said, "I will remember my song in the night . . ." (Psalm 77:6). The Psalmist was able to remember back to the time he was able to sing. He remembered the goodness of God in his life and how the joy of that goodness put a song on his lips. It was *that* song he chose to remember in the darkness of his spiritual unrest.

Jesus had a song in the night, as well. He sang that song with His friends. He was able to focus His heart and attention, not on His present and impending turmoil, but rather on the characteristics of His good and gracious Father. Read Psalm 118 and you will see that He sang lines such as, "Give thanks to the LORD for He is good." He sang, "His lovingkindness is everlasting." His song included, "The Lord is for me; I will not fear." He sang, "What can man do to me?" The night in which He was betrayed, Jesus sang, "The stone which the builders rejected has become the chief cornerstone." Jesus was able to take His eyes off Himself and focus them on His Father by singing His "song in the night."

Surely you and I will be able to take our eyes off ourselves long enough to focus on the wonderful attributes of our heavenly Father as well. Surely we will be able to remember our "song in the night." Quiet yourself long enough to remember back to that time in your life when the songs rolled easily from your lips. It is *that* song you and I are privileged to remember. The fact of the matter is this: Jesus' song in the night can be our song in the night. Read Psalm 118 if you don't believe me.

The Only Promise Kept

And Jesus said to them, "You will all fall away, because it is
written, 'I WILL STRIKE DOWN THE SHEPHERD, AND THE
SHEEP SHALL BE SCATTERED.' But after I have been raised,
I will go ahead of you to Galilee." But Peter said to Him,
"[Even] though all may fall away, yet I will not." And Jesus
said to him, "Truly I say to you, that this very night, before
a rooster crows twice, you yourself will deny Me three
times." But [Peter] kept saying insistently, "[Even] if I have
to die with You, I will not deny You!" And they all were
saying the same thing also.

MARK 14:27–31

❧

JESUS TRIED TO tell them that "the sheep" were about to scatter. By
quoting Zechariah 13:7, Jesus was predicting the failure or "stumbling" of His friends. The Shepherd was about to get ganged up on
by a pack of wolves, so to speak, and the sheep were going to do
what sheep do . . . run!

That's when the promises started being made. *I promise I won't
run! I can't speak for the others, but I will stand by you and with you!
Even if I have to die, I won't deny you!* None of those promises were
kept that evening and the next day. By the time the Passover meal
was complete and the last song was sung, it was probably close
to midnight. The disciples were giving up a good night's sleep for
Jesus. Surely they would continue the sacrificial living by standing
brave and tall once the wolves attacked. That is not, as you may
know, how it turned out. None of the promises the disciples made
that night were kept.

What kind of promises have you made to God? How easy has
it been for you to keep promises of loyalty, righteous living, or even
the leaving behind of a certain sin? How has your "sacrificial living"
been going lately? If you are like me, you have not done very well

with your promises to God. Just like the disciples, our intentions are pure as gold. When it comes to losing a little bit of sleep for Jesus, we are more than conquerors. It is when the stakes are raised and the temperature in the kitchen gets a little hotter that we start (quite surprisingly to ourselves, I might add) rethinking our position.

For the most part, we have a very romantic view of ourselves when it comes to loyalty to Jesus. We see in our mind's eye the warrior in us going toe to toe with the enemy. We see ourselves fighting the fight with such courage and strength that no foe is too formidable. We see ourselves wearing the mighty armor of God as we defeat the attackers. Maybe that is the problem Peter and his friends had that night; maybe they simply saw *themselves.*

It could be that if the disciples had listened more carefully, they would not have protested the truth and gone on to make promises they wouldn't keep. Jesus knew they were flawed human beings whose instinct for self-preservation would soon kick in. Jesus knew that He, as the great Shepherd, was about to be overtaken by the wolves. Jesus knew the sheep would scatter. That is why He made a promise to *them!* It was the only promise made that night that would be kept.

Read the passage carefully and you will see that Jesus promised, "But after I have been raised, I will go ahead of you to Galilee." This promise speaks to the power of God to raise the stricken Shepherd from the dead, but it speaks to even more than that. The promise made by Jesus that night speaks to the faithfulness of God to the weak and fearful men and women, like you and me, who are quick to make promises, and just as quick to break them. It is almost as if Jesus were saying, *I will go ahead of you to Galilee, meet me there and we will start over.*

In the midst of all our broken promises to God, we find the risen Shepherd keeping His promise to us. His faithfulness to us thrives even as our unfaithfulness to Him unfolds in the night. Let's rest in the promise of God to remain faithful to us in our stumbling and falling. When you think about it, of all the promises made that night, it was the only promise kept. Let's all (as sheep who have gone astray) rest on that promise from God as we seek to start over.

A Grieving Soul

They came to a place named Gethsemane; and He said to
His disciples, "Sit here until I have prayed." And He took
with Him Peter and James and John, and began to be very
distressed and troubled. And He said to them, "My soul
is deeply grieved to the point of death; remain here and
keep watch." And He went a little beyond [them], and fell
to the ground and [began] to pray that if it were possible,
the hour might pass Him by. And He was saying, "Abba!
Father! All things are possible for You; remove this cup
from Me; yet not what I will, but what You will."

MARK 14:32–36

✍

IT IS HARD to grieve. It is even harder to be with someone who is
grieving. What are we supposed to do? What are we supposed to
say? We often think it would help the grieving person if we let him
know he is not alone. We are tempted to say something along the
lines of, "I know how you feel because I once had the same thing
happen to me." The problem with that statement is that it is not
true. Everyone's pain is unique. Though certain events in life can be
common, the pain associated with the event is totally distinctive.
Our pain is our own. No one really knows how we feel. That's why
it is hard to be with someone who is grieving.

We see in this passage what a grieving soul is to do. We also see
how friends can respond to a grieving soul. Jesus has taught us that
a grieving soul prays while surrounded by friends. Have you ever
noticed the progression in the teaching life of Jesus? Jesus taught
and fed the *thousands*; He empowered and sent out the *seventy-two*;
He discipled the *twelve*; and He focused heavily on the *three* (Peter,
James, and John). It was this close group of three that He took with
Him, not only to the top of the Mount of Transfiguration, but also
deep into the garden to pray. These were the same three He took

with Him into the home of the little girl whom He raised from the dead. These guys were His close friends. They were the ones He asked to remain close to Him to keep watch. Jesus needed His friends surrounding Him in prayer.

Notice how Jesus was able to share His *feelings* with His friends. He revealed to them that His soul was deeply grieved. Only when the truth of how He was feeling was made known were His friends able to know how to pray. Notice, also, that Jesus was able to talk openly with God about His *desires*. He was honest in His petition. "Remove this cup" was an honest and specific appeal to have things happen a different way. This tells us that it is okay to be honest with God about our *feelings* and specific about our *requests*.

Jesus' prayer reveals another important insight into the needs of a grieving soul. He acknowledged both *intimacy with* and *dependency on* His Heavenly Father. "Abba" was the most intimate form of address a child could use in speaking with his father. It is the equivalent of our modern day title, "Daddy!" Jesus had such a close relationship with the Father that the title "Abba" was very natural. Keep in mind that grieving souls need intimacy with God. By acknowledging that "All things are possible for You . . . yet not what I will, but what You will," Jesus was showing His dependency on His Father. Jesus was trusting His Father's will and power in the midst of His own grief.

If you are grieving in any way right now, or if you know someone who is grieving, keep three things in mind. First, a grieving soul needs to be surrounded by friends who will "keep watch and pray." Allow your friends to hear how you are really *feeling*. Listen to how your friends are feeling and remember their pain is unique. Second, let God know your *requests*. Be specific. We are told to bring our desires to the Lord. Third, in recognizing the power of God to do all things, relinquish your desires to Him. Call for His will over yours. Because all things are possible for Him, we must trust His will and power in the midst of our own grief.

It is hard to grieve. It is even harder to be with someone who is grieving. If we were to follow Jesus through the process, we would keep our friends near, our requests specific, our hearts close to God's, and our wills second in line. We would also keep in mind that grieving is merely temporary. The resurrection reminds us of that wonderful truth!

Spiritual Sleepiness

And He came and found them sleeping, and said to Peter,
"Simon, are you asleep? Could you not keep watch for
one hour? Keep watching and praying that you may not
come into temptation; the spirit is willing, but the flesh is
weak." Again He went away and prayed, saying the same
words. And again He came and found them sleeping, for
their eyes were very heavy; and they did not know what
to answer Him. And He came the third time, and said to
them, "Are you still sleeping and resting? It is enough; the
hour has come; behold, the Son of Man is being betrayed
into the hands of sinners. Get up, let us be going; behold,
the one who betrays Me is at hand!"

MARK 14:37–42

JESUS WAS PRAYING in the Garden of Gethsemane while his friends
were supposedly watching and praying nearby. Jesus was with His
friends, but His friends were not with Him. Apparently His three
closest friends had become sleepy. His three closest friends were
not feeling His pain.

Jesus interrupted His prayer time three times to check on Peter,
James, and John. Each time He went to check on them He found
them sleeping. On the first visit Jesus took Peter to task, calling him
by his old name, Simon. It is interesting that He singled out Peter
though all three were sleeping. By using Peter's old name, Simon,
Jesus may have been giving him a strong hint as to the danger he
was in of falling back into the "old life" by being not just physically
sleepy, but spiritually sleepy at such a critical time. The battle ahead
was going to be fierce, and the soldiers needed to be awake.

How aware would you say you are of the spiritual battle that
rages just beyond your sight? Remember that the battle is a spiritual one, and thus it is invisible. If we are not careful we will walk

into the enemy's "sneak attack" unprepared for the fierceness of the fight. Peter was slipping back into his old ways which meant he was vulnerable to attack. It will take spiritual alertness (remember Christ telling His friends to be alert?). The eve of the attack is no time for sleeping.

Jesus interrupted His prayer a second time, and what He found was less than encouraging. They were asleep again! Their eyes were heavy and their tongues were tied. They could offer no good explanation for their lack of alertness. The passage says, "... they did not know what to answer Him." How many times have you found yourself "guilty as charged" when it comes to spiritual sleepiness, and thus have no defense? In my case, I have lost count. Spiritual failure does not just happen in a moment. Spiritual failure is a series of wayward steps that find their impetus from spiritual lethargy. If you and I don't stay awake at the wheel, we will surely crash. The lives of the disciples give testimony to this very fact. You would think that after two rebukes or warnings by Christ in this regard, they would have stayed awake. Such was not the case.

As we continue in the passage, we find them sleeping once again. The three times Jesus interrupted His prayer in the Garden of Gethsemane He found his friends sound asleep. What was going on with them? What is the problem with us? The problem lies within the heart of every spiritual man and woman. Jesus explained it by saying, "... the spirit is willing but the flesh is weak."

I do not think it is a coincidence that Peter was found asleep three times and he later denied Christ three times. I believe Peter took steps (deliberate or not) toward his failure. I believe we must acknowledge that the "bed" we make is the "bed" we must lie in, so to speak. If we allow the flesh to have its way in our lives we will experience spiritual failure.

Let's wake up! Let's open the Word of God and hear from Him. Let's stay spiritually awake as we man our posts on the battlefield. Let's keep communicating with our Commander. The enemy is awake, I can assure you. Jesus told His friends, and is telling us today, "Keep watching and praying that you may not come into temptation." Spiritual failure comes from spiritual sleepiness. Let's wake up!

To Be Brave

Immediately while He was still speaking, Judas, one of the
twelve, came up accompanied by a crowd with swords and
clubs, [who were] from the chief priests and the scribes
and the elders. Now he who was betraying Him had given
them a signal, saying, "Whomever I kiss, He is the one;
seize Him and lead Him away under guard." After coming,
Judas immediately went to Him, saying, "Rabbi!" and
kissed Him. They laid hands on Him and seized Him.
But one of those who stood by drew his sword, and struck
the slave of the high priest and cut off his ear. And Jesus
said to them, "Have you come out with swords and clubs
to arrest Me, as [you would] against a robber? Every day I
was with you in the temple teaching, and you did not seize
Me; but [this has] [taken place] to fulfill the Scriptures."
And they all left Him and fled.

MARK 14:43–50

❧

ALL OF US can be brave. Bravery is a part of our new nature provided by Christ. Difficult times can definitely produce fear in our
lives, but fear does not always have to win out in those difficult
times. Keep in mind that bravery is not the lack of fear. Bravery is
standing firm in the midst of fear. Someone once said it quite well,
"You can't be brave if you are not scared." The fact of the matter is
that all of us can be brave, but let's face it: there is also a coward in
us, as well. The definition of a coward is basically somebody who
is too easily or too greatly frightened. We see this kind of cowardly
response in today's passage. The question is, can we find ourselves
in today's passage? I am afraid so (no pun intended)!

The religious thugs followed Judas deep into the Garden of
Gethsemane to arrest Jesus in the dark of night. The coward in
them, as individuals and as a group, is obvious. Jesus pointed out

all the times they could have arrested Him in the Temple area since He had been teaching there almost every day that past week. The thugs were afraid of the crowd. They needed a time and place when Jesus would be less defendable. They needed a time and place when they could grab Him without a disturbance. If they had not been cowards, they would have arrested Him in public and in the light of day.

The disciples did not stand firm in the midst of fear, and thus acted cowardly as well. Once they realized that Jesus was not going to resist arrest, and once they realized one swing of the sword did not repel the mob, they ran. The final words of our passage are, "And they all left Him and fled." None of these events was a surprise to Jesus. He predicted the scattering of the sheep just hours before. The Scriptures (cf. Isaiah 53) predicted the way the mob would oppress Him, despise Him, and kill Him. If there is any surprise at all in the passages that follow, it would be the grace that is offered to cowards like you and me.

Consider the times you have allowed fear to drive you away from Jesus. Think about how many times you wanted to speak up at work or school about your faith, but decided not to because of fear of how you would be treated. Consider all the missed opportunities you have had to stay close to Christ, but the coward inside put on his or her running shoes and took off. It is hard to be a follower of Christ in this day and age. It is not what "everybody's doing." The only sin our society really recognizes these days is "intolerance." To walk closely with Jesus these days calls for courage (bravery) to resist many ungodly trends. We will be accused of being "intolerant" if we stick with Christ.

"Coward" is such an ugly word. No one wants to be a coward. We all want to be seen as the brave soul God created us to be. The spiritual life is definitely a "tug of war" between the *brave one* and the *scared one* in us all. As Paul reminded his young protégé Timothy, "For God has not given us a spirit of timidity, but of power and love and discipline" (2 Timothy 1:7). It will be the power of Christ in us that will keep us brave for Christ; it will be our love for Christ that will keep us close to Christ; and it will be the discipline of Christ in us that will keep us from leaving Him. It is not about fear. Remember, we can't be brave if we are not scared. All of us can be brave!

Running Away

A young man was following Him, wearing [nothing but] a
linen sheet over [his] naked [body]; and they seized him.
But he pulled free of the linen sheet and escaped naked.

MARK 14:51–52

❧

A YOUNG MAN followed Jesus and His friends deep into the Garden
of Gethsemane. The young man was nearly caught by those who
came to arrest Jesus. The detail of this young man running away naked is quite interesting and intriguing. No explanation is given as to
who this "young man" was or how he knew Jesus and His disciples
had gathered in that particular place.

There is a good chance, however, that the "young man" in this
account is John Mark. John Mark was the son of Mary, the owner
of the home that contained the "upper room" where Jesus had His
last supper before being crucified. It would make sense that John
Mark, having already gone to bed, could have been awakened as
Jesus and His friends finished the Passover meal, and not so quietly
went down the stairs and into the street. John Mark, who may have
been sleeping naked to ward off the night heat, may have climbed
out of bed and followed them wrapped only in the linen sheet he
was sleeping with. It could be that by the time he realized they were
walking across the Kidron Valley and onto the Mount of Olives, he
hit the "point of no return" for his clothes. Because the linen sheet
was an adequate cover, he followed them all the way to the Garden
of Gethsemane. This young man's running away naked is not the
end of the story. Before I tell you more of what happened in the
life of this young man, you may be interested to know that scholars
believe John Mark is also known as Mark, the author of this Gospel
account. This may explain how such detail was given.

John Mark (known as Mark in his later years) ended up being
a very strong, faithful, and brave follower of Jesus Christ. Keep in

mind, however, that he was not always strong, faithful, and brave. This recorded account in what is believed to be the life of John Mark shows that he was at first a *curious* young man without being a *committed* young man. Not until the resurrection of Christ do we even see the disciples fully empowered to hang tough with Jesus, so we need not be too hard on the young John Mark. John Mark had "running away" issues early on in his spiritual journey. Consider the account in Acts when, while on a missionary journey with Paul and Barnabas, John Mark ran away again. It seems that the mission field was tougher than he thought it would be. Luke writes, "Now Paul and his companions put out to sea from Paphos and came to Perga in Pamphylia; but John left them and returned to Jerusalem" (Acts 13:13a). In writing about the second missionary journey, Luke writes, "Barnabas wanted to take John, called Mark, along with them also. But Paul kept insisting that they should not take him along who had deserted them in Pamphylia and had not gone with them to the work" (Acts 15:37–38).

John Mark started out as a "runner," but that is not how he finished. Paul later wrote of the comfort and encouragement he received from Mark in his latter years. John Mark became a strong, faithful, and brave follower of Jesus Christ. Two things, I believe, worked in the life of John Mark over the years. One of those is grace. Grace is about lots of second chances. Grace is about forgiving the weaknesses and failures of the past. The second thing that worked in the life of John Mark was maturity. Maturity is about living more and more out of our brave heart and less and less out of our coward heart. If you have been "running away" from the difficulties of following Jesus, allow grace and maturity to work in your life. Allow the Lord to forgive you and give you many more "second chances," just as He did John Mark. Live more and more out of your brave heart and less and less out of your coward heart. Grace and maturity is what will move us beyond being *curious* and on to being *committed*. Yes, John Mark started off "running away" but that is not how he finished. The same can be true for you and me if we embrace the grace of God and let maturity develop in our strong, faithful, and brave hearts.

Wanting To Believe Lies

They led Jesus away to the high priest; and all the chief priests and the elders and the scribes gathered together. Peter had followed Him at a distance, right into the courtyard of the high priest; and he was sitting with the officers and warming himself at the fire. Now the chief priests and the whole Council kept trying to obtain testimony against Jesus to put Him to death, and they were not finding any. For many were giving false testimony against Him, but their testimony was not consistent. Some stood up and [began] to give false testimony against Him, saying, "We heard Him say, 'I will destroy this temple made with hands, and in three days I will build another made without hands.'" Not even in this respect was their testimony consistent. The high priest stood up [and came] forward and questioned Jesus, saying, "Do You not answer? What is it that these men are testifying against You?" But He kept silent and did not answer. Again the high priest was questioning Him, and saying to Him, "Are You the Christ, the Son of the Blessed [One]?" And Jesus said, "I am; and you shall see THE SON OF MAN SITTING AT THE RIGHT HAND OF POWER, and COMING WITH THE CLOUDS OF HEAVEN." Tearing his clothes, the high priest said, "What further need do we have of witnesses? You have heard the blasphemy; how does it seem to you?" And they all condemned Him to be deserving of death. Some began to spit at Him, and to blindfold Him, and to beat Him with their fists, and to say to Him, "Prophesy!" And the officers received Him with slaps [in the face].

MARK 14:53–65

THE MEN WHO had Jesus arrested and brought in for questioning had already made up their minds. They wanted Jesus dead but they needed two witnesses to testify to the accuracy of the charges against Him. The information, or testimony, they were looking for was information of a certain type. They weren't actually looking for truth; they were looking for blood. They were wanting to believe lies and they were wanting the people around them to believe them as well.

The Jewish laws were clear in that no one could be convicted without the testimony of at least two witnesses (cf. Numbers 35:30 and Deuteronomy 17:6). To be sure that justice was served, the law required the witnesses to be consistent. This is where the religious leaders (chief priests, elders, and scribes) were struggling. Their "expert" witnesses were not telling the same story. "For many were giving false witness against Him, but their testimony did not agree" (Mark 14:56). They were able, however, to find two people who said they heard Jesus say, "I will destroy this temple made with hands, and in three days I will build another made without hands."

It is interesting to note that the chief priests were not outraged when people stood shoulder to shoulder as they lied about Jesus. They did not tear their clothes in disgust over the kangaroo court proceedings. The multiple hearings during the multiple trials (religious as well as civil) did not have the discovery of truth as the ultimate goal. The ultimate goal was to get rid of Jesus, even if it meant rejecting the truth and even if it meant believing lies.

The chief priest stood eye to eye with Jesus and asked a wonderful question. As a matter of fact, if he had asked the question earlier in the evening, he would have saved everyone a lot of time. He asked, "Are you the Christ ... ?" (Mark 14:61) The answer to the question was just as wonderful. The answer Jesus gave was true and full of light and life. His answer laid out before the chief priest His true identity and function as the Son of the Blessed.

"I am," Jesus said. "I AM" is the Divine title of God Himself. It is the name Moses was to mention to Pharaoh in case he was asked who sent him. *You tell him that I AM sent you!* Jesus told the truth. The chief priest was questioning God Himself and yet was outraged at His answer.

Some people *want* to believe lies and are infuriated by the truth. Lies, they think, help them avoid the consequences of the truth. If

Jesus was truly God (I AM), and was going to be seen at the right hand of Power (I AM in charge), and will be coming with clouds of heaven (I AM going to bring justice), then the chief priest should have bent his knees rather than tear his clothes.

What about you and me? How are we doing with the truth? What areas of our lives must experience the bending of the knees before God Himself? Where have we failed to acknowledge His being in charge? What lies about Him are we holding on to? Some say He doesn't care and that He is a distant and uninterested God. Some lie and say that He will not forgive certain sins. Some of the lies we buy into are lies about His goodness, love, compassion, and mercy. When Jesus returns, as He promised He would, He will bring mercy, grace, love and justice. These truths about the great I AM are to be embraced. We must let go of the lies we have chosen to believe over the years. We must be willing to bend our knees in submission rather than tear our clothes in disgust. Let's no longer be a part of the crowd that is wanting to believe lies.

Embracing Our New Identity

As Peter was below in the courtyard, one of the servant-girls of the high priest came, and seeing Peter warming himself, she looked at him and said, "You also were with Jesus the Nazarene." But he denied [it], saying, "I neither know nor understand what you are talking about." And he went out onto the porch, and a rooster crowed. The servant-girl saw him, and began once more to say to the bystanders, "This is [one] of them!" But again he denied it. And after a little while the bystanders were again saying to Peter, "Surely you are [one] of them, for you are a Galilean too." But he began to curse and swear, "I do not know this man you are talking about!" Immediately a rooster crowed a second time. And Peter remembered how Jesus had made the remark to him, "Before a rooster crows twice, you will deny Me three times." And he began to weep.

MARK 14:66–72

WHEN PETER PUT his faith in Jesus three years earlier, he received a new identity. He was no longer the same man. Jesus changed him on the inside by giving him a new heart that was able to love God and remain loyal through times of trial and temptation. Jesus knew Peter would need that kind of heart throughout his life. The old heart would be able neither to love Jesus nor remain loyal. To remind Peter of his new identity, Jesus gave him a new name. He went from being known as Simon to being known as Peter. The question now is, Who showed up to warm himself by the fire that dark and chilly night? Was it Simon or was it Peter?

The servant girl knew Peter by his new identity and was announcing to those around her what she (and Peter) knew. The problem Peter was having that dark and chilly evening was embracing his new identity. It was his new identity that was drawing the attention of the hostile crowd. *This is one of them!* was not a statement he wanted to embrace at that particular moment.

Our old identity is made up of our flesh that will stand by anyone's "fire" just as long as it removes the "chill" brought on by sin. Our new identity is made up of the Spirit of Christ in us and knows that only Christ can remove the chilly effects of sin. Peter's dilemma speaks to our everyday struggle between our old and new identities.

Embracing and living out of our new identity is what the spiritual life is all about. Our old identity or "old man," according to Paul, loves to choose sides in a fight, gossip about people, meddle in the business of others, lust, cheat, grab, hate, and run away. As a matter of fact, the "old man" can do nothing but these things. Our new identity, or "new man" loves pursuing justice, showing mercy and kindness, seeking after peace, being patient with people, offering grace, and standing firm in the face of opposition.

Our denials of Jesus are no different than Peter's because they find their origin in our denial of the new identity given to us by Him. We *are* one of them! We *are* followers of Jesus! That is who we *are*! Why deny it? What are we trying to avoid by denying we belong to Him? Are we trying to avoid pain? Are we trying to avoid opposition? Do you remember the warning Jesus gave Peter in the garden? Do you remember that He told him about how the spirit is willing (new man) but that the flesh is weak (old man)?

The old man loves sin and will do nothing but embrace it when given the chance. The dark and chilly consequences of sin are real. Gathering around a man-made fire will not remove the ugly truth and consequences of our sin and denials. Only the warmth of Christ's graciousness and love will take away that damaging chill.

The new man hates sin and will do anything to avoid it when given the chance. The bright and warm consequences of life are just as real. Embracing our new identity will definitely result in opposition by those around us, but it will also result in the embracing of Jesus Himself. Once we learn to embrace the new identity given us by Christ, we will notice fewer and fewer instances of our failure to embrace Christ Himself (and vise-versa). The question still remains: Who will show up to warm himself by the fire on the dark and chilly nights that still remain? Let's be sure it is the "new man" rather than the "old"!

The Silence Of Submission

Early in the morning the chief priests with the elders
and scribes and the whole Council, immediately held a
consultation; and binding Jesus, they led Him away and
delivered Him to Pilate. Pilate questioned Him, "Are You
the King of the Jews?" And He answered him, "[It is as]
you say." The chief priests [began] to accuse Him harshly.
Then Pilate questioned Him again, saying, "Do You not
answer? See how many charges they bring against You!"
But Jesus made no further answer; so Pilate was amazed.

MARK 15:1–5

❧

JESUS HAD THREE hearings before the Roman authorities. You
would have to read the account in Luke to get the full picture but
basically Jesus went before Pilate, then Herod Antipas, and then
back to Pilate. In reading the accounts in both Mark and Luke, you
will find that Jesus said very little in His own defense. Mark records
the two short utterances of Jesus as He answered Caiaphas (Mark
14:62) and Pilate (Mark 15:2). Silence in a Roman court of law
was unusual. Defendants were usually quite vocal about their inno-
cence. Defendants usually defended themselves quite aggressively.
Knowing the way they could potentially die, defendants usually
spoke up. Jesus, however, said very little.

I believe the silence of Jesus says a lot. Under Jewish law, Jesus
was being accused of blasphemy, which carried the death penalty
as punishment. Under Roman law, Jesus was being accused of treason, which also carried the death penalty. Why did Jesus not defend
Himself? Why was He virtually silent in the midst of the "piling
on" of charges by the Sanhedrin? What was Jesus saying in His
silence?

Jesus' silence highlighted the fact that He, as the Son of Man,
was going to suffer at the hands of sinful man within God's sover-

eign plan. Jesus was demonstrating the silence of submission. His earlier prediction of being delivered over to the chief priests and the scribes, and being condemned to death (cf. Mark 10:32–33) contained a strong element of His own submission to it. He was not only declaring what was *going* to happen to Him but what He was going to *allow* to happen to Him. It was God's will for Him to suffer at the hands of rebellious and hateful men. It was God's will for Him to be the world's sacrificial Lamb. Submission to God's will demonstrates trust in God's will. Trust does not need a lot of words. Trust is a position one takes, not an argument one makes.

You and I are experiencing, at this very moment, the permissive will of God. He has us right where we need to be in order to demonstrate our trust in Him. The pain, sickness, emotional distress, and the sinful actions of people (including ourselves) that we are experiencing right now cannot be considered His *perfect* will for us but they are certainly His *permissive* will. The question we must ask ourselves is whether or not we are ready to trust God in the midst of the pain. Are we able to trust Him without feeling like we have to say a whole lot?

Again, trust is a position one takes, not an argument one makes. We can stand strong in the midst of personal injustice knowing that the King of kings and Lord of lords will one day make all things right. We can stand silent before our accusers knowing that the truth will one day be revealed and our acquittal will be real and complete. Our silence leaves room for the wrath of God. He is our defender; therefore we can obey the command not to repay evil with evil or insult with insult. We can turn the other cheek in silence because we are trusting God's permissive will.

Jesus' silence said a lot; therefore our silence can say a lot as well. Let's consider it the silence of submission.

A Son Of The Father

Now at [the] feast he used to release for them [any] one
prisoner whom they requested. The man named Barabbas
had been imprisoned with the insurrectionists who
had committed murder in the insurrection. The crowd
went up and began asking him [to] [do] as he had been
accustomed to do for them. Pilate answered them, saying,
"Do you want me to release for you the King of the Jews?"
For he was aware that the chief priests had handed Him
over because of envy. But the chief priests stirred up the
crowd [to ask] him to release Barabbas for them instead.
Answering again, Pilate said to them, "Then what shall I
do with Him whom you call the King of the Jews?" They
shouted back, "Crucify Him!" But Pilate said to them,
"Why, what evil has He done?" But they shouted all
the more, "Crucify Him!" Wishing to satisfy the crowd,
Pilate released Barabbas for them, and after having Jesus
scourged, he handed Him over to be crucified.

MARK 15:6–15

PILATE COULD NOT find a charge against Jesus worthy of the death
penalty. He thought he had a way out from behind the "eight ball"
by offering the stirred up crowd a choice. His assumption was, it
appears, that the people would choose to release Jesus instead of
Barabbas because Jesus was not a violent and ruthless killer like
Barabbas was. It may have been a "no-brainer" in his mind as to
whom the crowd would ask to be released, and so we can only
imagine the shock on his face when the crowd chanted Barabbas'
name.

The stirred up crowd was bloodthirsty and screamed, "Crucify
Him!" when Pilate asked what he was to do with Jesus. Pilate,
wishing to satisfy the crowd, let Barabbas go free and had Jesus

flogged and crucified. This, apparently, is not what Pilate thought would happen when he offered to repeat his tradition of releasing "for them any one prisoner whom they requested." His offer backfired. What Pilate didn't know was that Jesus was destined to die on a Roman cross that day, and Pilate's desire to satisfy the crowd would lead to that destiny.

Three crosses had already been built for that day's executions. Three criminals were sitting on "death row" and their crosses had already been prepared. All three of them deserved to die and it was only a matter of time until the nails would pierce their hands or wrists. (Sometimes the nails would be driven through the wrists because the flesh on the hands could easily tear away from the nails. Driving the nails through the wrists was a more secure way of crucifying someone.) One of the criminals sitting on death row that day was Barabbas. Barabbas was an insurrectionist. He was probably a Zealot who was able to lead a small uprising against the occupying Romans. In the midst of the fighting, people were killed. His crime carried with it punishment by death. Death by crucifixion. Barabbas deserved to die, but it was Jesus who ended up being nailed to the cross built for Barabbas.

You and I are Barabbas. You and I, if we were to be completely honest with ourselves, each other, and God, would have to admit that we have sinned against God. The Scripture helps us come to that realization as we read, "... for all have sinned and fall short of the glory of God ..." (Romans 3:23). We know that the death penalty applies to us as we read, "For the wages of sin is death ..." (Romans 6:23a). We are Barabbas.

Picture in your mind, if you will, a cross with your name pinned to it leaning against the wall. Realize that your rebellious attitude and actions have offended the Holy God of the universe, and your offense carries with it the sentence of death. Your cross has been built and you are sitting on death row. Imagine also, if you will, that as you sit in your cell, you hear your name being chanted, faintly at first but stronger as time goes on. Others in the cellblock realize it is your name they are chanting and confirm for you that you are not just hearing things. Imagine the door at the end of the hall opening and guards walking straight to your cell with key in hand. They use the key to open wide your cell door. They step aside and say, "You are free to go! You are being released. Someone else will be using your cross today."

Anyone who, by faith, allows Jesus to die on the cross that was meant for him experiences forgiveness. Forgiveness leads to adoption into the family of God the Father. "But as many received Him, to them He gave the right to become children of God . . ." (John 1:12). Consider the name, Barabbas. It is a compound word of *bar* meaning "son" and *abba* meaning "father." *Barabbas* means "son of the father." Those who watch, in faith, Jesus die on their cross become, in a mysterious way, *Barabbas* . . . son of the Father. Rejoice! You're free to go, for ". . . the free gift of God is eternal life in Christ Jesus our Lord . . ." (Romans 6:23b).

The Humiliated King

The soldiers took Him away into the palace (that is, the
Praetorium), and they called together the whole [Roman]
cohort. They dressed Him up in purple, and after twisting
a crown of thorns, they put it on Him; and they began to
acclaim Him, "Hail, King of the Jews!" They kept beating
His head with a reed, and spitting on Him, and kneeling
and bowing before Him. After they had mocked Him,
they took the purple robe off Him and put His [own]
garments on Him. And they led Him out to crucify Him.

MARK 15:16–20

THE BATTALION OF Roman soldiers had their fun at the expense
of Jesus. If it were a whole battalion of soldiers then there were six
hundred men (a tenth of a legion, which would be six thousand)
gathered around Jesus as He was being humiliated. If you have ever
been humiliated in front of one or two people then try to imagine
being humiliated in front of six hundred.

While skin was hanging off His back due to the scourging,
Jesus was dressed in a purple robe. The heavy material rubbed the
wounds as He was tossed back and forth among the soldiers. The
other Gospel writers add certain details to the event that help us
understand the extent of His humiliation. Having been blind-
folded, He was challenged to name the attackers. *If you are God,
then tell us who hit You? Hail, King of the Jews! Who wants to play
Who-Hit-The-King?*

Of course kings need a crown, so some of the more creative
soldiers fashioned a crown made of huge thorns. By pressing down
hard, the thorns were sure to gouge the scalp and cause profuse
bleeding. The *beating* of His body and face surely caused tremendous physical pain while the *mocking* of His person surely caused
spiritual and emotional pain. The humiliated King was in pain on a

physical, emotional, and spiritual level. Why? Why did Jesus allow Himself to be manhandled the way He was? Why did He choose to take it rather than dish it out? What kept Him from taking the mock scepter they had put in His hand and turning it on them with His Divine power and wrath? Why did the King allow Himself to be humiliated?

The answer to that question is difficult to communicate, partly because Divine love is difficult to communicate. How do we, as finite human beings, put words to such love? What dictionary exists that defines the depths of God's love for people who can be so viciously mean to one another and to Him? What thesaurus do we turn to for "another word for" such love? The fact that none exists is what makes communicating the reasons behind His humiliation so difficult.

Tearing a man's flesh off his body with a whip is awful. Beating, spitting, and mocking him definitely adds insult to injury, but we must keep in mind that Jesus allowed Himself to be humiliated in this way for a reason. If we do not take time to *embrace* the reason, we will never *appreciate* the reason.

I have decided that Divine love for a fallen human race cannot be expressed in words. In knowing that from the very beginning, I believe God planned on communicating His love not in words, but in action. What we would not and could not understand by *definition*, we would and could be able to understand by *demonstration*.

"But God demonstrates His own love toward us, in that while we were yet sinners, Christ died for us" (Romans 5:8). If a picture is truly worth a thousand words, then I am going to stop writing right now, get out of the way, and allow you to gaze upon the beautiful picture of Divine love. A picture I would like to entitle, *The Humiliated King: Divine Love Demonstrated.*

Embrace and appreciate God's love for you today!

From Passer-by To Servant

They pressed into service a passer-by coming from the
country, Simon of Cyrene (the father of Alexander and
Rufus), to bear His cross.

MARK 15:21

⨳

THE SON OF MAN was too weak to carry the crossbeam of His own
cross, which weighed an estimated one hundred pounds. The physical abuse had zapped Him of His strength. Having had no sleep
the night before, in addition to the flogging and beating, carrying
the cross proved to be too much for Jesus, the man. This passage
reminds us that Jesus was fully human and needed help.

This is when we meet Simon of Cyrene. Simon was a Hellenistic
Jew from the northern coast of Africa. He was more than likely entering Jerusalem as part of his pilgrimage from modern-day Libya.
He was a believer who was going to Jerusalem to honor the Lord
with his gifts and offerings. He was going to Jerusalem to celebrate
the Passover, which had been pointing to the coming Messiah for
hundreds of years. I doubt he expected to meet, much less serve,
the wounded and suffering Messiah he and other Jews had been
waiting for.

The detail of naming the sons of Simon lends tremendous
credibility to Mark's gospel account. Mark's Roman readers knew
his son, Rufus, from church (Romans 16:13). This account could
then be easily verified since names were mentioned. With the city
so crowded with pilgrims, finding housing in the city was probably
very difficult for Simon and his sons. Simon was thus "coming from
the country" where he was probably staying during the Passover
feast. It was while coming into town that Simon, the "passer-by",
became Simon the servant.

What did Simon learn about the Messiah in the midst of his
service? What does one learn about the Messiah when one watches

the way He dies? Simon did not see Him trying to escape His death but rather witnessed Him embracing it. Jesus did not return insult for insult. This must have had a tremendous impact on Simon as he served Christ. What did Jesus reveal about His own spirit as He silently went to the cross as a lamb to the slaughter? Jesus threw no punches at those who persecuted Him. What really happened to the inside of the pilgrim we know as Simon when he encountered the suffering Son of Man?

I think he learned what a true servant is.

What we learn about the Messiah by observing His suffering is that we can serve Him and others with the same character and spiritual resolve with which He served us. Just as Simon was pressed into service, we are called to serve as well. Will we be bitter? Will we throw insults and punches when those we serve insult and abuse us? Will we hate those we serve or love those we serve? Christ said Himself that He did not come to be served but to serve. Our marching orders are no different. We are to be servants of one another.

Let's not be deceived by appearances. Nothing is really by chance when God is involved. Simon was in the midst of celebrating the Passover (which included remembering the many lambs that were slain so that the believing slaves within Egypt could be saved from the spirit of death). Little did he know that he would be pressed into service on behalf of *the* Lamb of God who was too weak to carry His own cross.

Look around for those who are "too weak" to carry their own burden. Let's step up and serve as Simon stepped up to serve. Let's model ourselves after Christ who served without hate or bitterness. To be a servant is to be a person who dies to selfish gain and comfort. Jesus modeled this for Simon and for us. Let's model it to others as we are transformed from being a "passer-by" to a servant.

Unmasked Pain

Then they brought Him to the place Golgotha, which is translated, Place of a Skull. They tried to give Him wine mixed with myrrh; but He did not take it. And they crucified Him, and divided up His garments among themselves, casting lots for them [to decide] what each man should take. It was the third hour when they crucified Him. The inscription of the charge against Him read, "THE KING OF THE JEWS."

MARK 15:22–26

THE PHYSICAL PAIN of crucifixion was agonizing and horrendous. Crucifixion has been described as one of the cruelest forms of execution ever devised. The Romans did not invent it but they did develop it. *Unger's Bible Dictionary* points out that crucifixion, hanging both living as well as dead bodies from a pole, was utilized by the Egyptians, Carthaginians, Persians, Assyrians, Scythians, Indians, Germans, and Greeks, as well as the Romans. Crucifixion had a history. It also had a frightening reputation.

Crucifixion was a radical form of execution. It was reserved for the worst of the worst in the political, social, and religious cultures of the day. Jews associated the "hanging" of crucifixion with the curse of God. It is written, ". . . his corpse shall not hang all night on the tree, but you shall surely bury him on the same day (for he who is hanged is accursed of God) . . ." (Deuteronomy 21:23). Paul exposited this verse about crucifixion in his letter to the Galatians by writing, "Cursed is everyone who hangs on a tree" (Galatians 3:13b). Christ took on the full agonizing pain of crucifixion to become a curse for us all. Paul wrote, "Christ redeemed us from the curse of the Law having become a curse for us . . ." (Galatians 3:13a). Christ took the full brunt of unmasked pain.

There is an awesome truth (though often overlooked) found

in this passage that reveals that a numbing agent was offered to Jesus . . . and He refused it! Wine mixed with myrrh was soporific, that is, it was a drink that would cause drowsiness and then sleep. It was commonly given to those who were being crucified as an act of mercy. Proverbs 31:6 reveals this kind of mercy as we read, "Give strong drink to him who is perishing, and wine to him whose life is bitter." It was probably unheard of for a man to do anything but take in all that was given him. Christ, I believe, was trying to communicate something by refusing the drink that was meant to confuse His senses and deaden the pain of His suffering. What was He trying to communicate?

I believe Jesus was not only taking on the full brunt of the Law's curse but was taking it on willingly. By refusing the wine mixed with myrrh, He was communicating His desire to be fully aware throughout the torturous event. Unmasked pain communicates unmasked love. One cannot fully love if one is not willing to fully suffer. One cannot fully obey if one avoids the pain of that obedience. Jesus had the disposition to obey, but for Him to have the virtue of obedience, severe suffering was a necessity. Suffering leads to the virtue of obedience.

In laying down His life, Jesus was choosing to obey His Father's will. The sacrifice of His life on a Roman cross—a cross invented to inflict horrific suffering—was a visual display of love. It would have been a contradiction for Jesus to submit to the cross and not submit to the pain.

To say we are followers of Jesus and then to look for ways to avoid the pain of "dying to self" is just as much a contradiction. To mask the pain of discipleship with fleshly indulgence and selfish pleasures is to avoid the footsteps of the One we say we follow. Rather than masking the pain of our suffering for and with Jesus, we are called to embrace it for all the right reasons. Paul wrote to the Roman church, "And not only this, but we also exult in our tribulations, knowing that tribulation brings about perseverance; and perseverance, proven character; and proven character, hope . . ." (Romans 5:3–4). Endurance, character, and hope come by way of suffering through unmasked pain. Jesus is leading us that way. Are we following?

A Good Use Of Power

They crucified two robbers with Him, one on His right and one on His left. [And the Scripture was fulfilled which says, "And He was numbered with transgressors."] Those passing by were hurling abuse at Him, wagging their heads, and saying, "Ha! You who [are] [going to] destroy the temple and rebuild it in three days, save Yourself, and come down from the cross!" In the same way the chief priests also, along with the scribes, were mocking [Him] among themselves and saying, "He saved others; He cannot save Himself. Let [this] Christ, the King of Israel, now come down from the cross, so that we may see and believe!" Those who were crucified with Him were also insulting Him.

MARK 15:27–32

JESUS WAS HANGING on the cross because of our sin. The two criminals hanging on either side of Jesus were getting what they deserved, while Jesus was getting what you and I deserved. Jesus was hanging on the cross because His mission to pay for the sins of the world compelled Him to do so. The nails in His hands and His feet put Him on the cross, but there was something else that was really *keeping* Him on the cross. What was it?

Read the passage carefully and you will see two groups of people taunting Him. One group stood at the foot of the cross shaking their heads in scornful disapproval. They railed on Him as they challenged Him to use His power to come off the cross. The other group (the chief priests and scribes) ridiculed Him to one another saying He did not have the power to save Himself. The sarcasm was biting as they expressed their lack of faith in the power of Jesus Christ. To them, His hanging on the cross was a sign that He was a defeated "King" and a powerless "Savior."

Little did they know that Jesus was using His power to *stay on* the cross rather than to *come off* the cross. He used His power to fulfill His mission to pay for the sins of the world. He was even paying for the sin of blasphemy committed by those standing at the foot of the cross deriding Him as He suffered.

As believers, we have the power of the risen Christ inside of us. The salvation that was won for us by Christ remaining on the cross provides the power we need to live the redeemed lives we have been given. Our study of the resurrection will reveal more about this wonderful fact, but suffice it to say that the same power that kept Jesus faithful to His calling to die on the cross can keep us faithful to our calling to follow Him.

Think of all the things we are tempted to do with our power. We are tempted to "grab" rather than share. We are tempted to serve our own selfish desires rather than the legitimate spiritual needs of others. We are tempted to use our power to seek revenge rather than leave room for the wrath of God. There is tremendous temptation to use our power to advance our own will rather than the will of God. We are tempted to use our power to satisfy our flesh rather than live for the fulfillment of our spirit. I could go on.

I am thankful that Jesus did not react to the blasphemous taunting of those who did not believe in Him. I am glad that He used His power to stay on the cross rather than come down in a selfish display of force. The triumph of our Messiah eventually took place but not until the full brunt of God's wrath rested on His back. Staying on the cross was a good use of His power.

What will you and I use our God-given power to accomplish today? Will our power be used for selfish gain? Will our power be used to satisfy the flesh or glorify the Spirit? Jesus is not only our example in this but also our source. Let's not let the "voices" of the unbelieving world (physical or spiritual) taunt us to sin by trying to "prove" our worth. Our mission is to glorify God. This is a very good use of power, wouldn't you say?

The Shadow Of Death

When the sixth hour came, darkness fell over the whole
land until the ninth hour. At the ninth hour Jesus cried
out with a loud voice, "ELOI, ELOI, LAMA SABACHTHANI?"
which is translated, "MY GOD, MY GOD, WHY HAVE YOU
FORSAKEN ME?" When some of the bystanders heard it,
they [began] saying, "Behold, He is calling for Elijah."
Someone ran and filled a sponge with sour wine, put it on
a reed, and gave Him a drink, saying, "Let us see whether
Elijah will come to take Him down." And Jesus uttered a
loud cry, and breathed His last. And the veil of the temple
was torn in two from top to bottom. When the centurion,
who was standing right in front of Him, saw the way He
breathed His last, he said, "Truly this man was the Son of
God!"

MARK 15:33–39

FOR THREE HOURS the whole land was thrown into darkness. Jesus
was taking on the full brunt of His Father's wrath as He became
sin. "He made Him who knew no sin to be sin on our behalf, so that
we might become the righteousness of God in Him" (2 Corinthians
5:21). The darkness of judgment was real and the visuals provided
by God in the blotting out of the sun's light was a tremendous
sign of how serious the situation was. The only way to humanly
describe the agony of that judgment was for Jesus to use the word
"forsaken."

"Forsaken" best describes the separation our sin caused between the Father and the Son. Darkness, separation, and death are
summed up in Jesus' cry, "My God, My God, why have You forsaken Me?" Sin's terrible consequence hit Jesus hard. Sin's terrible
consequence hit Jesus like a speeding Mack truck.

Psalm 23 mentions the "valley of the shadow of death." King

David declared to the Lord that, "Even though I walk through the valley of the shadow of death, I will fear no evil, for You are with me ..." (Psalm 23:4). Notice that in "the valley of the shadow of death" there was no sense of forsakenness. The psalmist was able to sense the presence of the Lord at a very dark and dangerous time. What made the difference for David? Why did Jesus not sense His Father's presence?

There is a story told of a father and his little girl traveling together in the family car. As they were stopped at a stop sign at the intersection of a busy highway, a large Mack truck sped passed them at a high rate of speed. As the truck passed between them and the setting sun, the shadow of the truck quickly washed over them. The father asked the little girl, "Would you rather be hit by the shadow of the truck or the truck itself?" The little girl knew instinctively to reply, "The shadow of the truck, Daddy. It can't hurt us." The same is true for believers when it comes to the shadow of death. Only the *shadow* of death can touch the believer because Christ took the full brunt of sin's impact when He became sin and died.

The darkness, death, and forsakenness brought on by our sin hit Jesus like a Mack truck so that the *shadow* of death would pose no fear for us. Keep this in mind at the next funeral you attend. Those who die in Christ live even though they die. The hope of eternal life and the joy of forgiveness enable us to walk through the valley of the shadow of death without fear.

If you know someone who is afraid of dying, please share this Good News with him. If you know someone who has not put his trust in Christ's death on the cross, encourage him to consider responding to Him in faith. His willingness to be "forsaken" for us speaks to the depth of His love. Let's hold on to that wonderful love even as we travel in "the valley of the *shadow* of death" (emphasis added). "For the love of Christ controls us, having concluded this, that one died for all, therefore all died; and He died for all, so that they who live might no longer live for themselves, but for Him who died and rose again on their behalf" (2 Corinthians 5:14–15).

A Continued Faithfulness

> There were also [some] women looking on from a distance,
> among whom [were] Mary Magdalene, and Mary the
> mother of James the Less and Joses, and Salome. When
> He was in Galilee, they used to follow Him and minister
> to Him; and [there were] many other women who came
> up with Him to Jerusalem.
>
> MARK 15:40–41

NOT ALL THOSE who stood near the cross were unbelievers. Not all those who watched the slaughtering of the Lamb of God derided the sacrificial Lamb. There was a small group of faithful followers standing at the foot of the cross as they lived out a continued faithfulness.

Mark offers a short history or recap of the group's faithfulness by writing, "When He was in Galilee, they used to follow Him and minister to Him ... " (Mark 15:41). There were many others, he wrote, that followed Him to Jerusalem for the Passover. It could be that the entire crowd of faithful followers was, at that point, anticipating the establishment of His Kingdom. What was going through their confused minds and disappointed hearts as they saw Him arrested, beaten, and crucified is anyone's guess. If there was ever a time to "cut and run," that would be it. If there was ever a time to cease following and ministering, the scene in this passage would have been it. But this group of women did not cease following or ministering. They had a continued faithfulness.

What kept them faithful? Why did they stay close even as the majority of disciples disappeared from sight? It seems only John was close enough to hear from Jesus in His darkest hour. I believe their continued faithfulness came from a deep love and appreciation, which actually developed over time, for God's Messiah. The Messiah they put their trust in over the years was their Messiah in good times as well as bad times. Mary, who was from Magdala, was the one who had been freed from demonic bondage by her Messiah. The other Mary was the mother of James (the "little one") and Joses. Standing with those Marys was Mary, the mother of Jesus. We know about Jesus' mother being there from what we read in John 19:25. Salome, the mother of John and James who were the sons of Zebedee, stood with the other faithful ladies. It seems that they all had a personal, deep, and abiding love for Jesus that had started years before and continued on into the darkness of Calvary.

Do you trust yourself to remain faithful to Christ? Do your disappointments with God tempt you to abandon Him when things don't go well for you? How have you responded to God when He did not do for you what you thought He would or should? How would you describe the depth of your love and appreciation for Jesus right now? All of this matters as we reflect on the future because there is always a chance you and I can "disappear from sight," as the majority of disciples did, once disappointment with God hits.

The key to faithfulness in the future is faithfulness in the present. A steady and slow walk with Jesus allows us to know His heart and His desires. It allows us to trust Him in spite of how things may appear. It allows us to be passionate about His glory being revealed in the midst of the brokenness of life . . . ours included. Just as the faithful women of today's passage did not "cut and run" when the going got tough, let's remain just as faithful. I am convinced that He is calling us to a continued faithfulness in the midst of the pain!

The Courage To Get Messy

When evening had already come, because it was the
preparation day, that is, the day before the Sabbath, Joseph
of Arimathea came, a prominent member of the Council,
who himself was waiting for the kingdom of God; and he
gathered up courage and went in before Pilate, and asked
for the body of Jesus. Pilate wondered if He was dead by
this time, and summoning the centurion, he questioned
him as to whether He was already dead. And ascertaining
this from the centurion, he granted the body to Joseph.
Joseph bought a linen cloth, took Him down, wrapped
Him in the linen cloth and laid Him in a tomb which had
been hewn out in the rock; and he rolled a stone against
the entrance of the tomb. Mary Magdalene and Mary the
[mother] of Joses were looking on [to see] where He was
laid.

MARK 15:42–47

❧

MARK INDICATES THAT Pilate wanted confirmation that Jesus was
dead. Joseph had requested the body of Jesus but Pilate would not
release it to him until he was sure Jesus was dead. Pilate was surprised to hear that Jesus was not lingering. Jesus, according to the
centurion, was dead.

The historical records indicate that some men would hang on
the cross for several days.

Keep in mind that hanging on the cross restricted the use of
the diaphragm making it difficult to breathe. People who hung on
a cross had to push themselves up with their legs in order to take a
breath. Those on the cross had to get into a rhythm of pushing up
on the nail through their feet for as long as they could in order to
take a breath and then collapse back to hanging from their nailed
hands due to exhaustion. This would continue until they could no

longer push themselves up for a breath. There was a common practice of breaking the legs of those who lingered on the cross so that they would suffocate and die.

Jesus' legs did not need to be broken because He had already died. Pilate got the confirmation he needed from the centurion that was sent to check. It was only then that he allowed Joseph of Arimathea, "a prominent member of the Council," to retrieve the body of Christ. In reading John 19:38–39 we see that he and Nicodemus teamed up to remove the body from the cross. John indicates that Joseph was a disciple of Jesus, "but a secret one for fear of the Jews" and that Nicodemus was the one "who had first come to Him by night." What brought these two disciples out of the shadow of secrecy? What caused them to openly declare loyalty to Jesus by their efforts at caring for the body of Christ in the light of day? It was courage born of a faith willing to get messy!

Courage is "the ability to face danger, difficulty, uncertainty, or pain without being overcome by fear." Remember that courage is not the lack of fear. Courage is action in spite of fear. Consider not only the difficulty of proclaiming loyalty to Jesus by caring for His body, but also the amount of blood one would get on himself while taking a body off a cross. The picture of how "messy" it is to be a follower of Jesus could not be any clearer once you imagine Joseph and Nicodemus covered with Jesus' blood as they remove His body from the cross.

Following Jesus takes courage because following Jesus is "messy." All secret disciples must come out of the shadows and declare their loyalty with actions and not just words. We must all take courage, as Joseph did, and move close enough to Jesus to get messy. Messy spirituality is characterized by a willingness to confess sin, a commitment to let go of sin, a decision to obey Christ at all cost (social, financial, spiritual), and a commitment to serve Jesus and His friends (even the ones who are hard to love).

I believe the courage to declare love and loyalty on the part of Joseph and Nicodemus came from their seeing the sacrificial love and tremendous courage displayed by Christ's death on the cross. To embrace Jesus and His cross leads to the courage it takes to get messy for Him. Let's all do as Joseph did . . . let's all take courage! Let's all get messy!

He Has Risen!

When the Sabbath was over, Mary Magdalene, and Mary
the [mother] of James, and Salome, bought spices, so that
they might come and anoint Him. Very early on the first
day of the week, they came to the tomb when the sun
had risen. They were saying to one another, "Who will
roll away the stone for us from the entrance of the tomb?"
Looking up, they saw that the stone had been rolled away,
although it was extremely large. Entering the tomb, they
saw a young man sitting at the right, wearing a white robe;
and they were amazed. And he said to them, "Do not be
amazed; you are looking for Jesus the Nazarene, who has
been crucified. He has risen; He is not here; behold, [here
is] the place where they laid Him. But go, tell His disciples
and Peter, 'He is going ahead of you to Galilee; there you
will see Him, just as He told you.'" They went out and
fled from the tomb, for trembling and astonishment had
gripped them; and they said nothing to anyone, for they
were afraid.

MARK 16:1–8

THERE IS A definite odor that accompanies death. Once a body dies,
it begins to decay quickly and that rapid decay leads to a terrible
stench. Count yourself fortunate if you have never smelled the horrible odor of an animal's decaying body. It can turn your stomach.
Modern embalming techniques are used to combat rapid decay, but
Jewish society in the time of Christ did not use such techniques.
Therefore, the women in today's passage carried aromatic oils to
cover the stench of death. At least that is what they thought they
were going to do early on that long ago Sunday morning.

They knew where the tomb was because they saw Joseph and
Nicodemus bury Jesus on Friday afternoon. They knew there was

a large stone in front of the entrance, but apparently they were unaware of the other obstacles in their way. Obstacles such as the tomb having a Roman seal across it (a cord attached with wax so tampering could be detected) and Roman guards on watchful duty. These issues did not come up in their discussions. Their concern was merely a large and heavy stone that would need to be moved. It turned out there were no obstacles at all because of the power of God to break the seal, neutralize the guards, and remove the stone. Oh yes, and raise Jesus from the dead!

If God had not raised Jesus from the dead, the women would have needed the aromatic oils to cover the stench of death. Since that obstacle was no longer in front of them, the oils were no longer needed. While we have the science to combat the stench of physical death, I believe the stench of spiritual death continues to be a reality in the lives of people today. Without Christ, people are left to their own ingenuity when it comes to battling the obstacle of the spiritual stench of death.

Think about it—life stinks when marriages crumble, jobs are lost, friends and relatives die, valuables are stolen, lies are told and believed, fear dominates, and evil proliferates. Life stinks when dreams are shattered and promises are broken. Families are torn apart when fathers run away or mothers disappear (both physically and emotionally). The stench of spiritual death permeates the brokenness of life in every area. People are left to their own ingenuity when it comes to covering the stench of their spiritual death if Christ is not involved.

People carry a variety of "aromatic oils" with them just to cope with the stench. The preferred "spices" of the day are the abuse of drugs (including alcohol), or addiction to work, food, shopping, pornography, or sex. But what if, suddenly, there was no need to cover up the stench of spiritual death? What if the obstacles (real or imagined) were to miraculously disappear? What if the *seals, guards,* and *stones* that block us from Jesus could be moved away? What if death could miraculously be turned into life? If all that could happen, there would be no need for "spices" and "aromatic oils" to cover the stench of death.

All of this is summed up in the wonderful proclamation of the heavenly messenger who stood outside the tomb—"He has risen!" Death has been defeated. The stench of death is no more.

The power of sin has been broken; therefore the addictions we fall into to cover the horrendous smell of death are no longer needed. I would imagine the women tossed the aromatic oils into the ditch as they ran to announce the good news to the disciples. They no longer needed them to cover the smell of death. God defeated that "dragon." Because He has risen, you and I can toss our spices and oils into the ditch as well. They are no longer needed . . . for He has risen!

Publisher's note:
If you would like to be included on
John Wayland's Daily Passage e-mail list,
please send your request to whitecapsmedia@earthlink.net.
You can unsubscribe at any time.

Notes

Notes

www.ingramcontent.com/pod-product-compliance
Lightning Source LLC
LaVergne TN
LVHW011220080426

835509LV00005B/235